P

The Self Examined

"One of the important and difficult tasks of Christian educators and researchers today is to address issues related to identity and identity formation. *The Self Examined* proves a tremendous interdisciplinary resource for both the academy and all who want a nuanced and thoroughly Christian grounding in this important topic. As a university chaplain, this book has already been a great help in teaching and staff development. I highly recommend it."

—**Rob Rhea,** PhD, Chaplain and Director of the Centre for Spiritual Formation, Trinity Western University, British Colombia, Canada

"This book offers a variety of important contributions to the much-debated concept of identity. McGill gathers a group of professors, theologians, pastors, and practitioners from various disciplines, representing different cultural backgrounds, to consider aspects of human identity-making, articulating how multiple identities are negotiated and how self-understanding relates to Christian faith. It stands as an important contribution to the conversation of how and who we understand ourselves to be, and advances our discernment of identity, both in a biblical and in a broader cultural horizon."

—**Markus Zehnder,** PhD, Professor of Old Testament and Semitics, Talbot School of Theology

"These essays contribute new facets to the discussion of Christian identity, addressing topics such as shame, suffering, gender, forgiveness, and relationship in a way that is engaging and relevant. They are a rare combination of sound theory and robust theological discussion that lend themselves to devotional and life application. Each essay provides a rich, nuanced, balanced theological discussion that addresses important contemporary issues. It is a very timely and excellent contribution to our understanding of what it means to be created in the image of God."

—**A. Sue Russell,** PhD, Professor of Missions and Contextual Studies, Asbury Theological Seminary

"Identity may have taken the place of culture as the most complex word in daily use. For those of us called or responsible to assist others in their formation as Christians, exploring what it is, how it forms, and where it points is not optional. Fortunately, this new collection of essays offers rich and relevant discussions that will help readers makes sense of identity for their own Christian journeys as well for those contemporary issues where 'identity' is in play."

—**Todd Pickett,** PhD, Dean of Spiritual Development, Biola University

THE
SELF
EXAMINED

THE
SELF
EXAMINED

CHRISTIAN
PERSPECTIVES
ON
HUMAN
IDENTITY

JENNY McGILL
EDITOR

Abilene Christian University Press

THE SELF EXAMINED
Christian Perspectives on Human Identity

ISBN 978-1-68426-080-5 | LCCN 2018021659

Printed in the United States of America

LIBRARY OF CONGRESS CATALOGING-IN-PUBLICATION DATA
Names: McGill, Jenny, 1974- author.
Title: The self examined : Christian perspectives on human identity / Jenny McGill.
Description: Abilene : Abilene Christian University Press, 2018. | Includes bibliographical references.
Identifiers: LCCN 2018021659 | ISBN 9781684260805 (pbk.)
Subjects: LCSH: Identity (Psychology—Religious aspects—Christianity. | Identity (Psychology—Biblical teaching.
Classification: LCC BV4509.5 .M34345 2018 | DDC 233/.5—dc23
LC record available at https://lccn.loc.gov/ 2018021659

Cover design by Allshouse Graphic Design | Interior text design by Sandy Armstrong, Strong Design

For information contact:
Abilene Christian University Press
ACU Box 29138, Abilene, Texas 79699

1-877-816-4455 | www.acupressbooks.com

18 19 20 21 22 23 / 7 6 5 4 3 2 1

Contents

Acknowledgments

With a measure of trepidation, I assumed the responsibility for a writing project with nine contributors. This group of authors, however, has made this process joyous. I thank each of them for their expertise and insight, attitude, and diligence. My pleasure and sense of accomplishment comes from presenting their cogent thoughts to you, the reader. May our thoughtful expressions teach you, inspire you, and lead you into God our Father's will.

Many thanks are due to Abilene Christian University Press; its director, Jason Fikes; and managing editor, Rebecka Scott, with whom I worked; as well as to Sharon Duncan for her scrupulous editorial review of each chapter. Her review was made possible through a Lilly Faculty Scholarship Grant awarded to me by Indiana Wesleyan University during the preparation of this manuscript. My father, a chemist and physical scientist, shared in the project by his meticulous reading of this social scientific, theological work as a fellow scholar. I have long since appreciated his well-worn views on science and life. Lastly, nothing I endeavor is without the unfailing aid and constancy of my husband, Kevin. Any good I produce, apart from our Savior, is due in large part to him. I thank each of the authors again for their contributions to this work, and all of us would like to thank our triune God for recreating us and defining our Christian identity, which we now humbly convey to you.

Introduction

JENNY MCGILL

I am pleased to introduce this interdisciplinary and diverse work. *The Self Examined* presents a series of essays that examines themes of Christian identity in the Old and New Testaments, as well as contemporary visions of Christian identity amid current debates. Each author explores what a particular aspect of Christian identity entails and what it means for human flourishing. In this introduction, I will first offer a brief exploration of previous identity research, followed by definitions of key terms and a short summary of each chapter.

Theories of Identity

While space will not permit a recounting of the multitude of identity theories available, let me brush some very broad strokes. Regarding the concept of identity, psychologists more often focus on personal agency, while sociologists emphasize identity's social construction and highlight its institutional impact.[1]

Identity theories stem in part from a long history of scholarly exploration into the nature of the self. At the turn of the twentieth century, William James (1842–1910), along with Charles Horton Cooley and George

Herbert Mead, described an empirical self that was formed by social interaction. Symbolic interactionism, a term coined by Herbert Blumer to describe Mead's work, posits that people's actions are based on their interpretations, and social interactions create one's self-views. Far from the transcendent self, the empirical self is a social structure.[2] Sociologist Erving Goffman popularized the notion of the socially situated self in quotidian rituals.[3] In postmodern times, however, the very existence of the self is contentiously debated.[4]

Identity theories, while acknowledging both aspects of identity (individual and social), differ in their emphasis. Stryker's and Turner's identity theories focus on personal agency and self-continuity across situations. Others, such as Tajfel and Turner's social identity theory, emphasize how social factors affect individual perceptions.[5] After Erik Erikson's theory of identity development in the 1960s, racial identity theories began to flourish in the 1970s, followed by a host of distinctive, subject-specific identities (based on factors such as gender, disability, sexuality, and age).[6]

Most twentieth-century models do not effectively describe identity in multifaceted terms and tend to focus on one aspect of difference rather than on a combination of factors.[7] Like psychologist Dan McAdams, I hold that identity formation is a lifelong task that is refashioned and unfolds much like a story.[8] This narrative understanding of identity fits well with the theological framework of the story of God. A theological discussion of Christian identity in conversation with the social sciences has not been fully explored in the literature, and a continued discussion, therefore, is warranted. The authors, each in turn, discuss their understanding of identity and engage theology with their respective academic disciplines.

Key Terms

In order to provide a foundation for the chapters that follow, I must define, at least briefly, a few of the key terms that appear throughout this book. These include Christian, identity, and Christian identity.

Christian

Religious identity is usually defined by group affiliation or self-identification. Self-identifying criteria used by scholars, such as beliefs in biblical

literalism and an afterlife and the frequency of prayer and church attendance, have been employed to identify those of the Christian faith.[9] For
our purposes, the identifying label of Christian is rooted in the Greek
word εὐαγγέλιον, or *euangelion*, which means the gospel, or good news,
of Jesus Christ. The Christian gospel is to believe in Jesus Christ, the Son
of God. In believing in the Christ, one accepts that s/he has personally
betrayed the holiness and goodness of God and, through Christ's physical crucifixion, burial, and resurrection which appeased the wrath of God
on one's behalf, one's sin has been forgiven, one's connection to God has
been restored, and freedom to walk in a new life that follows the way of
Jesus has been initiated.

Identity

Identity has been defined as "the totality of a person's self-conception and
includes one's beliefs about oneself, one's roles, and one's group memberships."[10] One's identity-making is a process,[11] both fixed and fluid, that is
formed by one's socialization.[12] Identities can be ascribed with statuses
assigned by others (e.g., sex, race, age cohort such as "baby boomer," etc.).
Identity can also be achieved through statuses one adopts (e.g., educational attainment, occupation, and relationship, such as son-in-law, etc.).
Identities are forged by social structures and individuals, as people both
accept and deny characterizations based on their self-views.[13] Identities
can be examined as personal (one's self-perception), social (group membership), or collective (identity of a broader group).[14] In this work, the
authors use the terms "personal" and "individual" interchangeably.

Identity includes both a distancing from others ("who I am not") and
commonality with others ("who I am").[15] Any discussion of identity risks
harmful categorization, and the penchant to essentialize must be avoided.
Indeed, considering identity-making as story can help minimize this tendency, since a story contains the varied aspects of one's self-understanding
over the course of a lifetime.[16]

Christian Identity

While we acknowledge that identities are largely determined by individual and social imaginations, we believe that God speaks to shape human

identity (Gen. 2–3; Isa. 43:1). When a person accepts Christ's sacrifice on his or her behalf, one's self-understanding is not erased but redeemed. Previous identifications may be enlivened or discontinued; one's individual personality and talents are not lost. One's self-conception becomes sourced in Christ, and one's identities shift, and are even disrupted, into identification with Christ (2 Cor. 5:7). Identity-making becomes an act of faith (2 Cor. 5:7; Heb. 11:6). Self-views are reevaluated in light of one's new identity in Christ and membership in the body of Christ (Rom. 6:1–7, 20–22; 1 Cor. 6:9–12). Becoming a Christian requires a remaking, a renewing (Rom. 12:1–2; Eph. 4:23–24; Col. 3: 9–10; 1 John 3:3). Until the return of Christ, we will only know ourselves in part—who we think we are will be unimaginably changed (1 Cor. 3:9–15; 13:12; 1 John 2:17; 3:2).

Looking Ahead

In light of the other volumes that discuss the concept of identity at length within various fields such as sociology, psychology, and social psychology, we approach the concept from a religious and interdisciplinary viewpoint. In proposing possible themes for study, we passed over those that have been discussed at length elsewhere, such as human identity in the image of God and racial identity. Instead, we explore identity-making in terms of themes drawn from the Hebrew and Greek Scriptures and discuss Christian identity considering contemporary issues of our day. Part One considers identity in relation to human shame, love, forgiveness, and suffering. Part Two considers Christian identity in relation to migration, ethnic identity, embodiment, neurobiology, and gender. Since we realistically could not be exhaustive in our discussion, each author highlights their concept for further consideration.

In Chapter One, Jürgen Schulz considers the theme of shame in Genesis and recounts human identity before the corruption of the world (Gen. 1–3). He questions our culture's negative understanding of shame and proposes a more positive view of shame as a genuine human experience that functions as a protector of the ideal image of humanity. Schulz asks: What is shame? How is it understood in the Old Testament? What purpose(s) does it serve? How does shame shape and influence the ideal image of humanity and personal identity?

As my pastor often states, "Love for others is born from God's love for us."[17] In Chapter Two, Rod Reed discusses this theme of love in his analysis of the Gospel of Mark. Christian identity, especially among North American white evangelicals, is often defined by the intellectual content of one's beliefs. Such an understanding closely links following Christ with studying Scripture. In the Great Commandments (Mark 12:28–34), however, Jesus does not call believers primarily to an intellectual endorsement of the gospel. The Christian identity is primarily formed by the act of loving God and others with all of one's being. If a Christian's primary identity is as one who loves, then the process of sanctification must necessarily develop that person into becoming one who loves increasingly in daily life. The chapter then explores what the process of spiritual formation might look like if the church focused its efforts on helping members develop a primary Christian identity of love. As an exercise in practical theology, the focus moves from a theological exploration of such an identity to a discussion of the practices and attitudes that help foster such an identity. It also explores the dangers of replacing this primary identity of love, including contemporary examples of how an improperly focused Christian identity leads to imbalanced practices.

In Chapter Three, Célestin Musekura next explores the Christian identity of forgiveness as noted in Colossians. In Colossians 3:1–17, the apostle Paul reminds believers of what is required in order to live in peace. Since their identification with Christ through his death and resurrection seals their new identity, forgiveness is key to this new perspective and enables one to enter a new way of living. An identity of unforgiveness makes its owner twice a victim: first by her offenders and then by her own hatred. When Paul exhorts believers to think and behave in a new way, he reminds them that forgiveness sets them apart from the surrounding culture. Speaking from his personal knowledge and experience of the Rwandan genocide, Musekura describes how trust has been built among the widows of enemy tribes in a shared common interest. Colossians 3:1–17 confirms that when our tribal, racial, social, and economic identities are renewed by surrendering ourselves to Christ, our hearts and minds engage in actions that are supernatural. Putting on Christ enables believers to keep forgiving those who have sinned against them—even murderers. Christ in us makes forgiveness possible because through him and by God's Spirit our identity has been renewed for supernatural and divinely enabled actions.

Part One ends with Marc-André Caron's consideration of the thematic identity of suffering in Chapter Four. The book of Hebrews addresses a community that has experienced public shame, violence, theft, imprisonment, mistreatment, and even the threat of suffering and death. Caron explores the relationships between suffering, membership in the family of God, and personal behavior. Caron then addresses the primary question in relation to Christian identity: How does the theology of Hebrews—concerning the audience's familial links with God and each other—contribute to a Christian identity that will endure in faith despite society's attempts to terminate the Christian commitment? Like a father who consoles his child in a season of pain, God in Hebrews reassures his people and urges them to endure.

Part Two of this volume offers a series of conversations that address various contemporary identities and how they relate to one's religious identity as a Christian. The authors ask the question: How do these identities overlap, and how should Christians negotiate multiple identities? In Chapter Five, I start by describing how a theological understanding of Christian identity is migrant—a theology of identity that is specifically applied to the context of physical and spiritual migration. I then examine the identity of the converted Christian self in terms of the nature of its departure, belonging, and displacement.

In Chapter Six, Andrew B. Spurgeon discusses the intersection of ethnic and religious identity for East Asian Christian Indians. Because Christian congregants in India are caught in a cultural disconnect between colonial and postindependence India, the expressions of Protestant Indian Christianity often seem culturally irrelevant. In this chapter, following the model exemplified by the Indian government in refashioning the infrastructural face of India, the author describes a missional identity for Indian Christians as a way forward. Spurgeon offers a proactive, missional ministry approach that is infused with certain traditional and vital aspects of the Indian culture and addresses this primary question: How does one retain one's Indian cultural identity and live faithfully as a Christian?

In Chapter Seven, Lisa Igram takes up the question of how human physicality is crucial for Christian identity. Her chapter explores the following questions that surround our identity as embodied creatures: How was the human person and the human body defined within the Hebrew worldview of the New Testament? What might we discover if we feed our anemic understanding of the body by exploring a theological anthropology that is rooted in our God-created embodiment rather than in our God-given rationality? How might our Christian faith and practice develop if we elevated the value of our bodies to the level of our rationality and saw both as gifts from God our Creator? This chapter will explore nondualist readings of Paul and will consider how these perspectives elevate, for Western Christians, the value of the body to that of the mind. Finally, it will offer insights for practical Christian formation and discipleship based on a theology of our identity as embodied creatures.

In Chapter Eight, Andi Thacker continues the conversation in her discussion of the Christian identity and attachment. In the study of human development, the innate wiring for relationships is termed attachment, and one's attachment style is highly influenced by early childhood relationships. These relationships and, in turn, the framework developed from these relationships strongly influence one's attachment to God. This chapter will discuss human neurobiological development, the nature of attachment, its effect on personal identity, and how God influences such attachment and individual identity.

Finally, in Chapter Nine Nate Collins discusses a Christian view of gender identity. Within the fields of feminist and gender studies, the problem that multiplicity and difference pose to the concept of identity has spawned a wide range of approaches. Collins optimistically grounds gender identity in a physical reality in the outside world, even as he acknowledges that the knowledge of these realities is socially mediated and therefore subjective and incomplete. His chapter first outlines a critical realist approach to identity that can provide a foundation upon which an account of gender identity might be built. Second, he proposes a definition of personhood—created, relational, and historical—and explores how the relationship between first creation (Edenic) identities and Christian (new creation) identities affects our understanding of gender identity.

These contributors—who are theologians, administrators, psychologists, professors, and pastors—comprise a mix of voices from different continents, countries, and ethnicities. What we share is a common love for the triune God, and this love makes us a collegial family of sorts, brothers and sisters committed to God's restoration of this good earth. We offer you this work with the hope that it will help develop your own thoughts regarding the practice of Christian identity and, most importantly, draw you closer to the one true God.

NOTES

[1] Steph Lawler, *Identity: Sociological Perspectives* (Cambridge: Polity, 2014), 3.

[2] James A. Holstein and Jaber F. Gubrium, *The Self We Live By: Narrative Identity in a Postmodern World* (Oxford: Oxford University Press, 2014), 15.

[3] Erving Goffman, *The Presentation of Self in Everyday Life* (Garden City, NY: Doubleday, 1959).

[4] Consider the works of Galen Strawson, for example.

[5] Timothy J. Owens and Sarah Samblanet, "Self and Self-Concept," in *Handbook of Social Psychology*, ed. John D. DeLamater and Amanda Ward (2013), 482, 485, 488; Jonathan H. Turner, *Contemporary Sociological Theory* (Los Angeles: Sage, 2013), 331–55.

[6] Jenny Hyun Chung Pak, *Korean American Women: Stories of Acculturation and Changing Selves* (New York: Routledge, 2006), 10–12.

[7] Pak, *Korean American Women*, 15–17.

[8] Dan P. McAdams, *The Person: A New Introduction to Personality Psychology* (Hoboken, NJ: J. Wiley & Sons, 2006), 409–13.

[9] Duane F. Alwin et al., "Measuring Religious Identities in Surveys," *Public Opinion Quarterly* 70, no. 4 (2006): 539–40.

[10] Jenny McGill, *Religious Identity and Cultural Negotiation: Toward a Theology of Christian Identity in Migration* (Eugene, OR: Pickwick, 2016), 16–17.

[11] Luiz Carlos Susin, "A Critique of the Identity Paradigm," in *Creating Identity*, ed. Hermann Häring, Maureen Mieth, and Dietmar Junker-Kenny (London: SCM, 2000), 79.

[12] Richard Jenkins, *Rethinking Ethnicity: Arguments and Explorations* (London: Sage, 2008), 15.

[13] Jerry Z. Park, "The Ethnic and Religious Identities of Young Asian Americans" (PhD diss., University of Notre Dame, 2004), 21.

[14] Timothy J. Owens, "Self and Identity," in *Handbook of Social Psychology*, ed. John D. DeLamater (New York: Kluwer Academic/Plenum, 2003), 210–26.

[15] Lawler, *Identity*, 3–6.

[16] Dan P. McAdams, "The Redemptive Self: Narrative Identity in America Today," in *The Self and Memory*, ed. Denise R. Beike, James M. Lampinen, and Douglas A. Behrend (New York: Psychology, 2004), 99.

[17] Kevin McGill, quote taken from his sermon, Cornerstone Community Church, during the spring of 2017.

PART ONE

Themes of Identity in Scripture

An Identity of Shame in Genesis
The Human Condition

JÜRGEN SCHULZ

Every person must face matters of identity and shame, but a widely accepted definition of both terms is still wanting.[1] In this chapter, I will explore the nature and function of shame for the identity of an individual in the Old Testament, particularly in Genesis. In the texts of the Old Testament, we do not find a defined theoretical concept for identity in a modern or postmodern sense, and the same is true for shame. Shame is a genuinely human experience, and yet stereotypical assumptions about the nature and function of shame fall short because of the variations found between different cultures and languages. The understanding of shame in Germany and the United States—the two countries with which I am most familiar—differs significantly, for example. During our time in Dallas, I remember a debate in our student housing about the appropriate attire for women using the pool. For some, a bikini was considered to be too revealing and unacceptable. From my German beach experience, I was happy that they did not go topless. If two contemporary Western cultures already differ so greatly in their understanding of the same term (Eng., shame;

Ger., *Scham*), how should today's reader of the Old Testament understand what the text is saying when it uses the term? How, also, does shame function in the Old Testament in relation to the identity of the self? In the texts of the Old Testament, personal identity is closely connected with the social context of the self. In this connectedness, shame takes on an essential regulative function. This chapter seeks to explore these questions and varying aspects of shame. We begin with an exploration of the self in the Old Testament.

Identity: The Self in the Old Testament

The Old Testament does not contain specific technical terms that express the concept of "identity" or "person." How, then, do the Hebrew Scriptures speak of personal identity and the self, and how does our modern construction of personal identity connect with these ancient concepts? Using Charles Taylor's *Sources of the Self* as a gateway, I will first provide a sketch of our modern conception of self and then consider it alongside the Hebraic description of personhood.

Our contemporary Western languages use terminology that Charles Taylor, in his seminal work, locates in Plato's metaphor of Phaedrus in the classical Greek context. Here, identity is chiefly determined by a sense of inwardness.[2] For Taylor, the self is constituted by an "inside-outside" opposition, whereas the world within holds the key for finding the true self. Taylor explains:

> We think of our thoughts, ideas, or feelings as being "within" us, while the objects in the world which these mental states bear on are "without". Or else we think of our capacities or potentialities as "inner," awaiting the development which will manifest them or realize them in the public world. . . . We are creatures with inner depths; with partly unexplored and dark interiors.[3]

These "inner depths" are located within one's soul, the source of human thought and feeling, where reason should rule. Since it possesses the power of reason, the self is able to face the chaos of the outside world in a regulatory role.[4] Because of the dominance of reason, one's soul achieves within oneself a harmony that no longer depends on the outside world.

This notion of inner depths provides the foundation for the modern understanding of the self as an autonomous, disengaged, self-sufficient, and self-responsible unity. Individualism, as one of the prominent features of the modern identity, is an outgrowth of modernity's focus on the "inner depths." The self is grounded in one's "inside world" rather than in the "outside world" of one's social relations.[5]

In contrast, one of the fundamental and constitutive characteristics of the self in the Old Testament is its relationality and sociality.[6] Robert di Vito, in his comparison of Taylor's idea with Old Testament anthropology, points out these conflicting positions of inwardness and outwardness. He summarizes the concept of personhood as presented in the texts of the Old Testament with four aspects, thus identifying the very different construction of the self. Di Vito states that a person is

> 1) deeply embedded, or engaged, in its social identity, 2) comparatively decentered and undefined with respect to personal boundaries, 3) relatively transparent, socialized and embodied (in other words, altogether lacking in a sense of "inner depths") and 4) is "authentic" precisely in its heteronomy, in its obedience to another and dependence upon another.[7]

While some have emphasized the rule of reason as a constitutive factor of identity, the Old Testament presents a view of personal identity that focuses on constellations of complex relationships to the world outside of the self: to fellow human beings, to animals and plants, and also—in the transcendent realm—to God.[8] Relatedness is presented in the Old Testament as the "essence of man."[9] One's personal identity in the Old Testament is intertwined with one's social and collective identity. Di Vito goes so far as to emphasize a person's social context at the expense of his or her individual identity, a weakness in his otherwise very useful contribution.[10]

Now the question remains: How does the Old Testament speak about the individual personal identity as a self-contained entity, especially while taking into account the importance of the social context? Or is the notion of an individual self foreign to the Old Testament texts?

The anthropological aspects of a person are particularly expressed in the Old Testament through the usage of terminology for the body; bodily terms are central in conceptualizing humanity. In addition to their organic definitions, these terms carry socio-anthropological connotations and express relationality. See, for example, Psalm 16:7–10 (ESV):

> [7] I bless the LORD who gives me counsel;
>> in the night also *my kidney* (כִּלְיוֹתָי, *kilyôṯāy*) instructs me.
> [8] I have set the LORD always before me;
>> because he is at my right hand, I shall not be shaken.
> [9] Therefore *my heart* (לִבִּי, *libbi*) is glad,
>> and *my liver* (כְּבוֹדִי, *keḇôḏi*) rejoices;
>> my flesh (אַף־בְּשָׂרִי, *'ap-beśāri*) also dwells secure.
> [10] For you will not abandon *my soul* (נַפְשִׁי, *napši*) to Sheol,
>> or let your holy one see corruption.

The different body parts bring different aspects of the somatic and cognitive functions of the body into view: the kidneys (intuition), heart (reason), liver (emotion), flesh (the fugacity of life), and the soul (the neediness of humanity). These body parts are connected by verbs that express a course of action or emotion.[11] Only in relation to one another can we speak about the whole person who is drawing near to God (Ps. 16).

The reference to individual body parts is thus a reference to the body's relational function. Through the body, relationships between fellow human beings and God are established. The soul, for example, is misunderstood if we interpret it in a dualistic sense, as an entity separate from the body. The word denotes "vitality" or "vital energy" that is not found in itself but in seeking relatedness—a relatedness to God (Ps. 16). The term *soul* labels someone with a need for relationships.[12] Schroer and Staubli go so far as to state, "This *nephesh*-ness of the human being means that we are entirely oriented to relationship, from the very beginning."[13] The living aspect of the self, in its capacity to relate, is the core meaning of the soul. What is relevant for the term *soul* is also applicable to other body parts, a matter that will need to be discussed elsewhere. For our purpose, it is important to have in mind that in the Old Testament the relationality of a person is so fundamental that it is grounded in the body itself.[14]

Each body term emphasizes one aspect of a person but also must be understood in its totality. For the anthropology of the Old Testament, it is important to focus not only on the unique feature of each aspect or what has been called elsewhere the "principle of the aspective," but also on the "principle of the connectivity." The connectivity of these individual aspects can be described with the help of the concept of a "constellative construct."[15] As with the human body, the whole is seen through the constellation of its individual aspects. Without this inherent relationality, the whole is unthinkable.

In the Old Testament, anthropology is portrayed in a multidimensional fashion, presenting corporeality and relationality as essential characteristics of the self. Personal identity is another facet of this multidimensionality. Bernd Janowski, who rejects Di Vito's description of the self as "decentered and undefined with respect to personal boundaries,"[16] situates the individual identity in the heart (לֵב/ לֵבָב, *leb/lebāb*), which he calls "a symbol for the 'inner person.'"[17] Contrary to the modern understanding, the Hebrew concept of the heart is the center of cognition. But in the Old Testament, the emotional and volitional aspects are also located in the heart. All three merge and are difficult to separate from one another.[18] The experiences of the reciprocal relationship between the inner and outer world of the self are located in the heart. To examine the self in the Old Testament by focusing solely on the social context and the external world means to neglect the whole person. Old Testament anthropology must understand the individual not only within the social context, but also as an individual identity. The world within and the world without have to be viewed in tandem.

The interrelation of corporeality and sociality are constitutive for personal identity. The personal and social dimensions are connected, as can be seen in the human body; the body is a union of individual parts. Comparatively, the personal self is part of a collective such as a family household or ethnic group. The individual and the collective do not merely coexist but depend on each other, and the personal is always correlated with the collective.[19] This understanding of the self stands in contradiction to the concept of corporate personality most often seen in Old Testament studies, which perceives the individual exclusively through the group with a concomitant neglect of his or her individual aspects.[20] The Old Testament does acknowledge the individual self and presents it as one dimension of an identity concept.

In Old Testament studies, another unique dimension of the self is its relation to the supernatural. The personal identity is embedded in its sociality—a sociality that, at its core, carries a religious-transcendent element.[21] The individual in the Old Testament is predominantly presented as one part of a chosen collective: the people of Israel. As part of the chosen nation, the individual is related to YHWH, the divine. Although this relationship can also be observed for the individual apart from the people of Israel (e.g., Jonah and Nineveh), a qualitative difference for the individual who is part of the chosen nation exists. Only Israel, in contrast to its neighboring nations, is regarded as the people of God, a nation with an established direct relationship with the divine.[22] The personal self of the Israelite is part of a sacred people, and it is only by belonging to the divine that the self is complete.[23] The identification of the individual with the collective, and the collective's acceptance of the individual, is constitutive for an Old Testament anthropology.[24]

The Hebrew concept of identity differs significantly from modern Western ideas. To present the personal identity as an alternative to the collective would be an anachronism. Multidimensional relatedness is fundamental. The physical, social, personal, and religious-transcendent dimensions are deeply intertwined. The personal self is embedded in the collective, and the collective is constituted by the individual.

Shame, by its very nature, is both a personal and a collective experience. Before we review the different aspects of shame in relation to identity, however, we will explore its meaning in the Old Testament.

The Concept of Shame in the Old Testament

The Hebrew verb בוש (bôš) in Genesis 2:25, which is usually translated "ashamed," serves as a key term in the garden narrative of Genesis 2–3. Since a major investigation of the concept of shame for ancient Israelites through the lens of theological and historical anthropology is lacking, it is essential to understand the words that describe shame.[25] Thus far, only limited research has been done on the actual meaning of the different "shame words" in the Old Testament. While a comprehensive semantic contribution is beyond the scope of this chapter, it is necessary to define the concept of shame in the Old Testament and examine its use in a larger discussion of identity.

The three major shame words in the Hebrew text—בוש (*bôš*), כלם (*klm*), and חפר (*ḥpr*)—are generally translated as "to shame" or "to put to shame." They express either a generic connotation that describes the experience of shame in general or a personal connotation of the particular feeling. The challenge faced in reading a translation of the Old Testament is the loss of context and nuance. The concept is more multifaceted than the lexical definitions suggest.[26] A comparison between different dictionary entries reveals further nuances in meaning. "To humiliate, to hurt," for example, is (according to some) the prioritized and preferred translation for the verb כלם (*klm*).[27] When we take into account the different order of meaning in the dictionaries, "shame" is only listed as second or third in importance. It can be argued that the feelings of being hurt and humiliated can be interpreted as expressions of shame, but to actually use the word "shame" in a translation is likely to lead to a loss of nuance present in the concept of the word.[28]

The exact relationship between the concepts of humiliation and shame must be determined at another time, but it is important to recognize that shame and humiliation are linked and that this link is important for the definition of בוש (*bôš*). The parallel usage of primary shame words shows that it is not possible to separate the subjective aspect of feeling ashamed from the objective aspect of being humiliated (Isa. 26:11; Ps. 40:14).[29] A closer examination of the derivatives of בוש (*bôš*) provides helpful insights; they "embrace both aspects, from disgrace, worthless(ness), to shame" (Deut. 25:11; Jer. 3:25; Ps. 35:26).[30] To humiliate, to undo someone, or to feel ashamed are all connected with the motifs of worthlessness and nothingness.

In a religious context, the objective, transitive aspect of "shame" is dominant. In the prayer of Psalm 31, the psalmist asks for protection, while his enemy should be destroyed—be put to shame (v. 17). This request is connected with the motif of trust. Since the enemy does not trust God and is thus not connected with the divine, they have no protective relationship and are vulnerable to destruction and annihilation. Those who act against the will of God will be destroyed. The term בוש (*bôš*) thus speaks about an experienced distance from God, a life lived without divine aid.[31] This experience also holds true outside of a religious context. As soon as social and other expectations are not met, someone might experience בוש (*bôš*) (2 Sam. 19:6). This might occur in an objective sense by an external humiliation or by a subjective feeling that is caused through self-awareness of one's own shortcomings. Behind both senses is a motif of unmet expectations or guilt.

Furthermore, בוש (*bôš*) is what someone experiences after a loss, which leads to the breakdown of one's social status, as Seebaß explains: "בוש [*bôš*] means . . . the human emotion of shame, the failed ideal, the shattered state of a once ecstatic condition."[32] Here again appears the idea of unmet expectations and a failed ideal. When expectations and reality do not match, the result is disgrace. The meaning of בוש (*bôš*), however, extends beyond disgrace. "To do somebody injustice" (2 Sam. 19:6) or "to do wrong against God" (Hosea 9:10) are other nuances Seebaß notes. For Israel to act against God pulls the rug out from under their feet, so to speak. They lose the power that secured their safety and well-being (Isa. 20:5).[33] They are embarrassed—which results in the emotional effect of shame.

Shame is consequential; a moment of unmet expectations or guilt precedes the feeling. בוש (*bôš*) is the disgrace Israel experiences. While they could have been an esteemed nation, a wrong act by the people of Israel or by an individual, either in the eyes of a significant other or before God, causes the experience of בוש (*bôš*).[34]

In parenting, the "experience of shame" can easily be observed. Children often try to push boundaries. They are not content with the "family rules" that have been set up for their good. Take, for example, a task as innocuous as tooth brushing. One evening, one of my children looked me in the eye and claimed that he had brushed his teeth, but his toothbrush was still dry. As I confronted him about my unmet expectations, his body language revealed his shame, and he could no longer look me in the eye. As his father, I contested his lie and challenged his wrong act. Since parental opinion is central to a child's identity formation, being convicted by parents is particularly serious.

According to Philip Nel, the meaning of shame is always correlated with a negative condition, an experience where perceived standards (such as a code of conduct or a set of expectations linked with one's position or family relationships) are not fully met. Someone experiences בוש (*bôš*) because he or she reasonably fears to have violated standards of "decency or correct conduct."[35] Martin Klopfenstein, in his analysis, also emphasizes the proposed link between shame and guilt: "'Shame' and 'disgrace' indicate guilt, and the subjective feeling of being ashamed implicitly reveals a consciousness of guilt and with that remorse."[36] The motif of guilt does not require a religious context, such as one that acknowledges sin—an idea worthy of inquiry but that goes beyond the scope of this project. Every unmet expectation, every deviation from the expected, can cause shame and disgrace.[37]

According to the current state of research in the study of the concept of shame, a definition of shame must begin with a reference to guilt and/or honor. The concept of בוש (*bôš*) and its equivalents, however, is multifaceted. Shame functions as a semantic category to describe a wide range of meanings. The motifs of worthlessness and nothingness, unmet expectations and guilt, and honor and trust play a vital role in the experience of shame. Thus far, a definition that connotes the complexity of shame in the Old Testament has not been expounded.[38]

Today's readers and interpreters of the biblical text need to bear in mind the different dynamics in the biblical concept of shame where guilt and honor will be a returning point of reference. Shame is a genuinely human, multifaceted, dyadic experience between fellow human beings and/or God that is caused by a divergence from perceived expectations. From this discussion of the meaning of shame in the Old Testament, let us move on to the function of shame for the construct of identity in ancient Israel.

The Function of Shame for the Self in the Old Testament

The importance of shame in ancient Israel can be seen in its prominent placement in Genesis 2–3. In a perfect, Edenic world, the concept of shame is unheard of. Genesis 2:25 states, "And the man and his wife were both naked and were not ashamed." This verse summarizes the preceding paragraph (v. 21–24) and offers the only portrayal of the human condition in the garden, the one place where all the negative and destructive aspects of life are yet unknown. As the perception of human identity changes, the human condition of shame is introduced. Human identity and the function of shame hinge on Genesis 2:25.

Verse 25 leads into the next passage in Genesis 3:1–7. Here the focus shifts from the creation account to Adam and Eve's expulsion from the garden, and the full meaning and weight of Genesis 2:25[39] becomes more apparent:

> Then the eyes of both were opened, and they knew that they
> were naked.

Through this retrospective, the tension of verse 25 becomes clear: both were naked and were not ashamed [before each other]. As my translation indicates, I understand the verb form to be reflexive and reciprocal.[40] The relationship between the first man and first woman is initially an unburdened relationship. The dyadic nature of shame—the distancing of the self in response to the negative reflection of the other and the fear of being seen by the other—is not yet experienced. This perfect relationship is highlighted in the preceding verses (v. 21–24). As the naming indicates, the man beautifully relates himself to the woman; she is called אִשָּׁה (iššāh), woman, because the man, אִישׁ (iš), relates to her (v. 23). He sees himself in her and yet also sees something altogether incredibly different and mysterious in her. She is his truest counterpart.

The biblical text portrays relatedness as a genuine human necessity (v. 20), and humanity is incomplete until the introduction of woman.[41] Through God's gift of a counterpart, Adam experiences a relationality and sociality without equal.[42] Through the process of naming, he fully understands not only his own personal identity and individuality, but also the Otherness of the self in the opposite sex and how they are both necessarily embedded within a collective.

In Genesis 2:25, both man and woman are naked, and in their openness toward one another, they are equals. This nakedness without shame indicates a human condition free of the desire for any status symbols (Ger., *Statuslosigkeit*). Both relate perfectly and are content with the status quo (which soon turns into a relatedness filled with desirous tension by Gen. 3:6, 16). Most importantly, this nakedness expresses an openness toward God. The absence of shame is, as Hartenstein puts it, an "expression of an undisturbed fellowship—still without any break or crack (also regarding the relationship to God)."[43] Genesis 2:25 then describes the ideal image of human identity: perfect individuality in relationality. Our identity is found in our uniqueness and also in our relationship to those with whom we are connected. Here, man and woman complement each other without fault. Neither the horizontal relation between two humans nor the vertical relation between human and God are disrupted. The self is whole when in a reciprocal relationship with the other.

Genesis 3:7, a composite of phrases from Genesis 2:25 and 3:5, illustrates a human's capacity for cognition (Ger., *Erkenntnisfähigkeit*) in correlation with an awareness of shame (Ger., *Schambewusstsein*). The verb *knew* (ידע, *yāda'*) expresses the cognitive aspect and precedes the emotional expression of shame (Gen. 3:10, ירא, *yārē'*, to fear). The emotive aspect is not an expression of an inner state detached from the outside world. Rather, through the inner emotion of "I was afraid [אִירָא, *'irā'*], because I was naked" (v. 10), a person acts outwardly and hides (Gen. 3:10). Precisely in this moment of shame, the nature of human identity as relational—both internal and external, both personal and social—becomes clear. Self-confidence shatters with embarrassment.[44] Relational ease erodes into hiding from the other. Human identity, one's understanding of who one is, is lost. From this moment, mutuality collapses and one's personal identity stands in conflict with one's collective identity. Relational distance demands a covering (Gen. 3:21). The first-person use of the three verb forms in verse 10 ("I heard" [שָׁמַעְתִּי, *šama'ti*], "I was afraid" [אִירָא, *'irā*], "I hid myself" [אֶחָבֵא, *'ehābe'*], ESV) and the personal pronoun אנכי (I [*'ānōki*]) stress the individual's egoism. One's personal identity, one's wholeness, becomes incomplete. Human identity, as individual and related, becomes driven by fear.

In this new awareness of humanity's nakedness, shame should not be equated with the discovery of sexuality. In fact, the sexual orientation and complementing character of the different biological sexes is affirmed (Gen. 2:23) before shame is mentioned (v. 25). Since בוש (*bôš*) has no clear sexual connotation, it would be misleading to focus in this context on the sexual aspect of shame. The knowledge of good and evil expressed by the verb ידע (yāda', to know) is not used in reference to a sexual act here. Even the term עָרוֹם ('ārôm, nakedness) is not exclusively sexual. Nakedness, rather than representing sexuality, is rather an expression of a life that is free of any status or hierarchy.[45] Alexandra Grund goes so far as to see two entire independent lines of development in one's sexual maturity and emotion of shame—the one is strictly separated from the other. If this claim holds true is a matter for further research.[46] Considering that verse 25 is a summary, the awareness of one's sexuality is affirmed as genuinely human and not part of an experience of shame. A discussion about identity and shame has to overcome the strong association of the latter with guilt or disgrace, as it is given in the English language. A negative evaluation of sexuality from the shame described in Genesis 3 does not do the text justice.

To deny a connection between the motifs of guilt and shame altogether also goes too far.[47] As the couple experiences shame for the first time, they perceive themselves as guilty for the first time. Their new awareness of their nakedness signals their vulnerability before God (Gen. 3:7), a vulnerability that has been caused by their divergence from the expected, the motif of guilt. This divergence is manifested explicitly in their hiding because of their nakedness (v. 10–11). Life in the perfect world, free of any status rivalry and hierarchy, and therefore free of any shame, has come to an end. The downside of the new cognition of good and evil (Gen. 2:17; 3:22) is manifested in the experience of shame. This experience reveals to the first couple their vulnerability and then their guilt. Or as Seebaß puts it, "Their sense of the need for protection from their Creator is stronger than the sense of the violation of God's decree."[48] The desire for protection occurs because of the awareness of an unmet expectation, indicated by feeling a sense of shame. Shame per se is not a negative emotion or experience, but here it does indicate the negative and signal a moment of guilt.

Shame in itself is not a symptom of guilt and sin but is directly associated with the cognition of good and evil. Shame is not negative per se, but it emphasizes the new cognitive aspect, which includes the awareness of the negative. Shame serves a regulative purpose in a world of good and evil. Shame is a "dowry of Eden,"[49] for a life marked by disturbed fellow-ship. Shame points out the imperfect, the divergence from what should be, and the moments of guilt that follow. Thus, through shame a life *post lapsum*—after the fall—maintains an awareness of the Edenic conditions. Westermann's observation that shame should be understood as a protection from evil is therefore an important contribution to our understanding of the function of shame.[50] To manage life in the imperfect world, shame is vital.

Outside of Eden, a life without shame is unheard of; it is a genuinely human condition. Someone who becomes shameless loses part of what makes him or her human, part of his or her identity. The positive aspect of shame, which serves in life management and aids in the avoidance of evil, appears many times in the prophetic literature, where "shame words" are used most frequently next to the wisdom literature. God rebukes the nation of Israel with an accusation that points out their loss of shame (Jer. 6:15) or by shaming them to raise their awareness of their guilt (Ezek. 36:32).[51]

Since life's circumstances are often the opposite of an undisturbed, Edenic fellowship, shame can signal or warn the self about the danger of dishonor. In the Psalms, life under distress is frequently characterized by a description of personally held shame (Ps. 14:6), but the one who does not hide in fear but takes refuge in God will not be ashamed (Ps. 25:2–20). In this imperfect world, the fear of being shamed by others can be frightening, but when acceptance and recognition by God is of the highest importance, this fear can be overcome.

Application

What, therefore, do we learn from the regulative role of shame in the Old Testament, and how can we apply this to a dialogue about identity in a (post)modern age? I offer three considerations and one caution.

Shame, first of all, informs us that something is amiss. We live, theo-logically speaking, in a world post-fall. In our daily lives, shame pricks our consciences when something is not as it should be. A moment of felt shame—because we have failed to live in accordance with our own expec-tations, within the core values of our community, or within the confines of what we believe in—can provide the chance for change; we can choose to turn from what is not right to what is good. Shame challenges us to bring back into balance what is causing the turmoil we experience, either inwardly in our conscience or outwardly in our social context. Thus, from a Christian perspective, shame is a healthy mechanism and references the general revelation given to humanity (Eccles. 3:11; Rom. 1).

Shame, secondly, protects us from harmful intrusion. The moment that we experience shame potentially points to a harmful situation—my identity, myself, I am in danger. Sadly, we live in a world where people damage the self, the privacy, of others. Social harm is an intrusion into one's identity, one's most personal space, and it is experienced through shame. Authentic shame can serve to protect us from those who would do us harm. Cultivating a strong sensitivity for shameful situations will help protect one's own identity from malevolent intrusion.

Lastly, shame can regulate the closeness of human relationships. Our identity is primarily created in relationship to others. Shame regulates these relationships, for example, indicating potential harm or, positively, indicating great virtue. In a virtuous relationship, our shame sensitivity decreases since we are not in need of protection from the other. The growing openness leads to a growing vulnerability as a bond of trust forms. Betraying this trust is, therefore, even more painful and disastrous.

As a caution, ignoring or rejecting one's experience of shame can mean losing part of what makes us human.[52] Shame is a genuine human emotion and an experience that needs to be cultivated and protected. In the Old Testament, shame is clearly linked with the covering of one's nakedness. Admittedly, every culture has its own understanding of what is appropriate, and every generation has to wrestle about this appropriateness anew. Yet, if in this fight, the sense of shame in connection with one's nakedness is lost altogether, part of what makes us human—with the resulting protection of our identity—is forfeited as well. Our body is not only in danger; our self-understanding is (Matt. 10:28; Luke 12:4–5).

Summary
Human self-perception changed after sin corrupted the world (Gen. 3). The core motif of the emotional experience of shame in Genesis 2 and 3 makes this tension visible. While the understanding of the (post)modern

concept of personal identity—its inwardness and individuality—is key, identity is also constructed, according to the Old Testament, as intimately relational and embedded within a collective. Genesis 2:25 bridges the Edenic and post-Edenic world and introduces a fundamental anthropological experience: one's appropriate sense of shame in one's existence before God. An identity of shame was unnecessary and nonexistent in the early, undisturbed fellowship between man and woman and God. With Genesis 3:7, shame became a human reality, and one's identity, one's self-understanding changed. Relationality, what it means to be human, was challenged. The relationship between man and woman and God was disrupted, in which shame now plays a vital regulative function. When one becomes shameless, he or she loses a part of his or her humanity. Shame, the awareness that something is not right in the world, is the dowry from Eden for a life in this imperfect world. As painful as it is, it will be needed until the world is restored (Rev. 21–22).

NOTES

[1] Markus Öhler, "'Identität'—Eine Problemanzeige," in *Religionsgemeinschaft und Identität: Prozesse jüdischer und christlicher Identitätsbildung im Rahmen der Antike*, ed. Markus Öhler (Neukirchen-Vluyn: Neukirchener Theologie, 2013), 9.

[2] Robert Di Vito, "Old Testament Anthropology and the Construction of Personal Identity," *The Catholic Biblical Quarterly* 61, no. 2 (1999): 220.

[3] Charles Taylor, *Sources of the Self: The Making of the Modern Identity* (Cambridge, MA: Harvard University Press, 1989), 111.

[4] "By its domination [the rule of reason] the person achieves within himself or herself a kind of unity or harmony, a centering within oneself that prevents one from being driven by conflicting desires." Di Vito, "Old Testament Anthropology," 221.

[5] Di Vito, "Old Testament Anthropology," 220.

[6] Jan Dietrich, "Human Relationality and Sociality in Ancient Israel: Mapping the Social Anthropology of the Old Testament," in *What Is Human? Theological Encounters with Anthropology*, ed. Eve-Marie Becker (Göttingen: Vandenhoeck & Ruprecht, 2017).

[7] Di Vito, "Old Testament Anthropology," 221.

[8] Dietrich, "Human Relationality," 23.

[9] Michaela Bauks, "Neuere Forschungen zum altorientalischen Seelebegriff am Beispiel der Anthropogonien," in *Anthropologie(n) des Alten Testaments*, ed. Jürgen van Oorschot and Andreas Wagner (Leipzig: Evangelische Verlagsanstalt, 2015), 113; Dietrich, "Human Relationality," 24.

[10] All quotations originally in German have been translated by the author. Bernd Janowski, "Wie Spricht das Alte Testament von 'Personaler Identität'? Ein Antwortversuch," in *Konstruktionen individueller und kollektiver identität (I): Altes Israel/Frühjudentum, Griechische Antike, Neues Testament/Alte Kirche*, ed. Eberhard Bons and Karin Finsterbusch (Göttingen: Vandenhoeck & Ruprecht, 2016), 34.

[11] Bernd Janoswki, *Konfliktgespräche mit Gott: Eine Anthropologie der Psalmen*, 3rd ed. (Göttingen: Neukirchener Theologie, 2009), 8–9, 44. For a detailed list of examples of body terms and their functions, see Dietrich, "Human Relationality," 25–26; Janowski, "Wie Spricht das Alte Testament," 36.

[12] Hans Walter Wolff, *Anthropology of the Old Testament*, 2nd ed. (London: SCM Press, 2012), 10–25.

[13] Silvia Schroer and Thomas Staubli, *Body Symbolism in the Bible* (Collegeville, MN: Liturgical Press, 2001), 58.

[14] Taylor, in his description of the modern conception of the self, also refers to body terms in order to describe best how we perceive ourselves: "So we naturally come to think that we have selves the way we have heads or arms, and inner depths the way we have hearts or livers, as a matter of hard interpretation-free fact." Taylor, *Sources of Self*, 112.

[15] Bernd Janowski, "Anerkennung und Gegenseitigkeit: Zum konstellativen Personbegriff des Alten Testaments," in *Der Mensch im Alten Israel: Neue Forschungen zur alttestamentlichen Anthropologie*, ed. Bernd Janowski and Kathrin Liess (Freiburg: Herder, 2009), 184.

[16] Janowski, "Anerkennung und Gegenseitigkeit," 184, footnote 8 and 11.

[17] Janowski, "Wie Spricht das Alte Testament," 37.

[18] Janowski, "Wie Spricht das Alte Testament," 39–50.

[19] See the discussion in Dietrich, "Human Relationality," 28.

[20] See John W. Rogerson, "The Hebrew Conception of Corporate Personality: A Re-Examination," in *Anthropological Approaches to the Old Testament*, ed. Bernhard Lang (Philadelphia: Fortress Press, 1985), 43–59.

[21] Marianne Grohmann, "Diskontinutität und Kontinuität in alttestamentlichen Identitätskonzepten," in *Religionsgemeinschaft und Identität: Prozesse jüdischer und christlicher Identitätsbildung im Rahmen der Antike*, ed. Markus Öhler (Neukirchen-Vluyn: Neukirchener Theologie, 2013), 36.

[22] See Horst Seebaß, "Israels Identität als Volk des Einen Gottes," in *Religion und Identität: Im Horizont des Pluralismus*, ed. Werner Gephardt and Hans Waldenfels (Frankfurt: Suhrkamp, 1999), 87.

[23] Janowski, "Wie Spricht das Alte Testament," 58.

[24] Dietrich introduces the term *mutual social identity*, but in this chapter, I will continue to use *collective identity*. See Dietrich, "Human Relationality," 28–30.

[25] Yael Avrahami, "בוש in the Psalms—Shame or Disappointment?," *Journal for the Study of the Old Testament* 34, no. 3 (2010): 298.

[26] See David J. A. Clines, *The Dictionary of Classical Hebrew, Volumes 1–8* (Sheffield, UK: Sheffield Phoenix Press, 2011); Wilhelm Gesenius, Rudolf Meyer, and Herbert Donner, *Hebräisches und Aramäisches Handwörterbuch über das Alte Testament* (Berlin: Springer, 2013); Ludwig Köhler and Walter Baumgartner, *Hebräisches und Aramäisches Lexikon zum Alten Testament (HALAT)*, ed. Walter Baumgartner, Johann Jakob Stamm, and Benedikt Hartmann, 3rd ed., vol. 1 (Leiden: Brill, 2004), 130–32, 289, 426–27.

[27] Köhler and Baumgartner, *HALAT*, 457.

[28] Gary Stansell, "Honor and Shame in the David Narratives," *Semeia* 68 (1996): 61.

[29] F. Stolz, "בוש," in *Theological Lexicon of the Old Testament*, ed. Ernst Jenni and Claus Westermann (Peabody, MA: Hendrickson Publishers, 1997), 204–8.

[30] Stolz, "בוש," 206.

[31] Avrahami, "בוש in the Psalms," 303.

[32] Horst Seebaß, "בוש," in *THWAT*, ed. G. Johannes Botterweck, Helmer Ringgren, and Heinz-Josef Fabry (Stuttgart: Kohlhammer, 1973), 571.

[33] Seebaß, "בוש," 573.

[34] Seebaß observes that YHWH judged his people for the sake of truth: "The destruction, which is linked with disgrace, is in its result not disgrace but demonstration of the uniqueness of [YHWH]." Seebaß, "בוש," 577.

[35] Philip J. Nel, "בוש," in *The New International Dictionary of Old Testament Theology and Exegesis*, ed. Willem A. Vangemeren (Grand Rapids, MI: Zondervan, 1997), 613–14.

[36] "It remains, 'shame' and 'disgrace' indicate guilt and especially the subjective notion of being ashamed imply consciousness of guilt and with it remorse." Martin A. Klopfenstein, *Scham und Schande nach dem Alten Testament: Eine begriffsgeschichtliche Untersuchung zu den hebräischen Wurzeln bôš, klm und ḥpr* (Zürich: Theologischer Verlag, 1972), 208.

[37] Klopfenstein's conclusions have been questioned, namely for his theological bias, in Avrahami, "בוש in the Psalms," 297; Lyn Bechtel-Huber, "The Biblical Experience of Shame/Shaming: The Social Experience of Shame/Shaming in Biblical Israel in

Relation to Its Use as Religious Metaphor" (PhD diss., Drew University, 1983), 45–55. No alternative research on the definition of shame words, however, has been presented. Aware of the bias of his work, here I follow Klopfenstein.

[38] Such a variety cannot be covered in a typical lexical dictionary, where we look for the equivalent in the modern language of the one ancient word.

[39] Author's translation.

[40] Gesenius, Meyer, and Donner, *Hebräisches und Aramäisches Handwörterbuch*, 134.

[41] Wendy Alsup, "Apologetics for Women," *Fathom*, July 17, 2017, https://www.fathommag.com/stories/apologetics-for-women-1. See also Gerhard von Rad, *Das Erste Buch Mose: Genesis*, vol. 9 (Göttingen: Vandenhoeck & Ruprecht, 1972), 39.

[42] Bernd Janowski, "Konstellative Anthropologie: Zum Begriff der Person im Alten Testament," in *Biblische Anthropologie: Neue Einsichten aus dem Alten Testament*, ed. Christian Frevel (Freiburg: Herder, 2010), 70.

[43] Friedhelm Hartenstein, "'Und sie erkannten, daß sie nackt waren' (Genesis 3,7). Beobachtungen zur Anthropologie der Paradieserzählung," *Evangelische Theologie* 65 (2005): 286.

[44] Claus Westermann, *Genesis* (Neukirchen-Vluyn: Neukirchener Verlag, 1974), 341.

[45] Hartenstein, "Und sie erkannten," 292.

[46] Alexandra Grund, "'Und Sie schämten sich nicht' Zur alttestamentlichen Anthropologie der Scham im Spiegel von Genesis 2–3," in *Was ist der Mensch, dass du seiner gedenkst (Psalm 8,5): Aspekte einer theologischen Anthropologie*, ed. Michaela Bauks (Neukirchen-Vluyn: Neukirchener Theologie, 2008), 119.

[47] Bechtel-Huber, "Biblical Experience of Shame," 45–55.

[48] Horst Seebaß, *Genesis I: Urgeschichte (1,1–11,26)* (Neukirchen-Vluyn: Neukirchener Theologie, 1996), 123.

[49] This term is borrowed from Grund, "Und Sie schämten sich nicht," 121.

[50] Westermann, *Genesis*, 342.

[51] Jacqueline E. Lapsley, "Shame and Self-Knowledge: The Positive Role of Shame in Ezekiel's View of the Moral Self," in *The Book of Ezekiel: Theological and Anthropological Perspectives*, ed. Margaret S. Odell and John T. Strong (Atlanta: Society of Biblical Literature, 2000), 157.

[52] See Wright's provocative musing in N. T. Wright, *Surprised by Hope: Rethinking Heaven, the Resurrection, and the Mission of the Church* (New York: HarperOne, 2008), 181–83.

An Identity of Gospel Love

The Centrality of the Second Great Commandment for Christian Identity

ROD REED

W hen students and faculty at the university where I work come into my office to discuss their spiritual problems, the script is often familiar. When I ask what troubles them, they usually talk about one of three categories of issues. Some struggle with a lack of discipline in "spiritual things" such as prayer, Bible study, or church attendance. Others struggle with sexual issues such as pornography use, premarital sexual intimacy, or sexual orientation. Still others wrestle with difficult intellectual issues such as the problem of evil, creation/evolution, or the exclusivity of Christ. To my recollection, however, I have never heard anyone identify their spiritual problem with one of the following statements:

"I'm concerned that I'm a jerk to my roommate."

"I don't treat my professor with respect, and I think it's a spiritual issue."

"I think that my anger is driving my kids away from me."

What's more, I've certainly never heard someone complain that their concept of Christian identity might be at fault for the spiritual problems they experience. Could it be, however, that the struggles these students and faculty experience are more reflective of a misaligned sense of identity than they are of a deficit in self-discipline or resistance to temptation? Specifically, could the lack of a transformed Christian life say more about where we locate our spiritual identity and how we expect God to change us than it does about our commitment to pursuing "spiritual things?"

Maybe our vision of spiritual maturity and identity is too limited and needs to include different indicators of Christlikeness that focus more on relationships than on self-discipline. For example, one marker of my own spiritual maturity might be whether my wife and kids are happy when I come home at the end of the day, because they don't have to worry about what to expect if it's been a bad day at work. In other words, could the tone of voice that my kids use when they say, "Daddy's home," be one indicator of Christlikeness for me? Or, could the way that people who disagree with Christians feel loved by us be a better indicator of Christlikeness than how much Scripture we know? Many of Jesus's stories and interactions in Scripture seem to indicate at least the possibility of relational indicators of Christian faithfulness.[1] Of course, it is not necessary to choose between loving others and faithfulness to Scripture, but if we do not see loving others as a primary reflection of God's impact on our lives, we risk minimizing the transformative work that the Holy Spirit seeks to do in us. We also risk minimizing the impact of the gospel in a world that is increasingly hostile or apathetic to the truth of Scripture.

When we look at the life of Christ, we see many excellent attributes, but chief among them is an unsurpassed quality of love. His love for the rich and the poor, the powerful and the powerless, his friends and his enemies, distinguished him from any other teacher or prophet. We rarely think of Christ engaging in theological debates about esoterica, even though his understanding of and commitment to the Hebrew Scriptures were unsurpassed. While what he believed was crucially important, Jesus continually challenged people to consider that faithfulness to God inherently focuses on an embodied love that affects all those who encounter his followers. Richard Averbeck states, "When we walk with Jesus according to His likeness, being transformed into His image, nothing else makes any sense . . . except to go love God and people."[2] C. Stephen Evans adds, "Even without a command from God, the person who loves God has a reason to love all humans, because one cannot truly love God and not love what is made in God's image."[3] If this is true, Christians' personal and social identities should prioritize love for others as a primary indicator of spiritual maturity.

In this chapter, I want to explore the very familiar teaching from Mark 12 that we call the "Great Commandments." In particular, I want to focus on the primary verb—to love—that Jesus uses to call Christians to faithfully follow him. I will argue that this verb indicates a clear center of identity for the Christian life that looks very different from a belief-centered identity or a behavior-centered identity. The goal of this critique is not to diminish the importance of Scripture, behavioral purity, or spiritual practices, but to locate them within a relational identity that is rooted in Christ's love.

As a work of practical theology, I will explore the theological foundations for pursuing such an identity and will provide practical methods for doing so. Additionally, I will follow the common practice in practical theology of first-person usage and narrative examples of praxis. The starting point for this critique addresses the need to see love as an issue of identity.

Why Identity?

If an identity of love is central to the Christian life, it is important to understand what this identity looks like. First, as discussed in the introduction to this book, identities are not possessions but are states of being that are socialized in unique ways. My evangelical tradition, for example, socializes its members by emphasizing the following four characteristics:[4]

- Biblicism (the Bible as authoritative for belief and practice)
- Crucicentrism (the centrality of Christ's sacrifice on the cross)
- Conversionism (the necessity of conversion for salvation)
- Activism (Christians are to work hard in the Christian life, especially in evangelism.)

These characteristics set the parameters for an evangelical identity and also set the trajectory for what spiritual maturity within evangelicalism looks like. Like all ecclesiastical identities, it brings with it certain potential "blind spots" and unintended consequences. For example, while the emphasis on the authority of the Bible advances a reliance on Scripture, it also creates the possibility for unbelievers to perceive evangelicals as people who are more concerned with correct belief than compassion for those in pain. Consequently, evangelicals in the United States today are often perceived as unloving, bigoted, or hateful because of the way they communicate their commitment to the authority of Scripture.[5] For Christians who desire to be faithful to Scripture and Christ's work on the cross, this perceived identity seems at odds with our core mission. Is it possible for Christians to remain firmly committed to the truth of Scripture and still be known as an inherently loving people?

Making love an issue of identity is crucial for Christian faithfulness and for the perception of Christians by others. It is not merely a matter of changing some beliefs or trying to be more loving. We need to cultivate an identity that reflects Christ in a way that intrinsically influences everything we do, because our actions flow from our identity. James K. A. Smith states, "Our wants and longings and desires are at the core of our identity, the wellspring from which our actions and behavior flow."[6] Smith echoes the message of Augustine of Hippo here as he contemplates the impact of love, both ordered and disordered, on the life of the Christian. Augustine taught that the holy person is not simply the one who does what is right, but whose life reflects the priority of love given by God. He states,

> Now he is a man of just and holy life who forms an unpreju-
> diced estimate of things, and keeps his affections also under
> strict control, so that he neither loves what he ought not to love,
> nor fails to love what he ought to love, nor loves that equally
> which ought to be loved either less or more, nor loves less or
> more which ought to be loved equally.[7]

In other words, Christian identity, rightly understood, emphasizes the centrality of appropriately ordered loves. If we do not address the core of our identity, our actions will not reflect Christ, who embodied perfect love.

Dallas Willard states this in a different way: "If I do evil, I am the kind of person who does evil; if I do good, I am the kind of person who does good. Actions are expressions of who we are. They come out of our heart."[8] Seeing Christian maturity as a reflection of appropriately ordered loves changes the way that we envision spiritual identity. However, it is essential to understand that this process is impossible apart from God's grace and power, as the Apostle Paul reminds us in 2 Corinthians 3:5: "Not that we are competent in ourselves to claim anything for ourselves, but our competence comes from God." In addition to being saved by grace, the believer is completely reliant upon God's grace for his or her continued spiritual formation. Aquinas explores these themes in depth in *Summa Theologica* and concludes that apart from grace we are unable to comprehend truth, will or do good, love God, fulfill the commandments, avoid sin, or persevere in faith.[9] God calls us to pursue these things, but only as a secondary response to his initiative of grace in our lives. Consequently, we strive for an identity of rightly ordered love, but cannot consistently change our actions until we allow the Holy Spirit to change the core of our being so that we reflect Christ's identity of love in all that we do.

Pope Francis provides a good example of how to locate theological convictions within an identity of love. Since assuming the papacy in 2013, he has become wildly popular around the world, even though the Catholic Church has not changed any major doctrine since his ascension. I contend that his popularity is directly related to the way in which he loves people in unexpected ways. When he kissed a leper (November 6, 2013), he communicated something central about the gospel apart from any papal encyclicals. When he embraced a Muslim Imam (April 28, 2017), even as he called for Muslim leaders to stand against violence, he indicated a different way of living out his beliefs that is compelling to an unbelieving world. He communicates the love of Christ by acting lovingly. He embodies Christ's love for God and others by expressing compassion for those on the margins of society, as well as by advocating for peace, calling upon those in power. Pope Francis illustrates Alistair McGrath's point that "[t]here must be no mismatch or contradiction between the message that is proclaimed and the messenger's proclamation. We must be winsome, generous and gracious."[10] The tone with which we speak and the medium by which we communicate the gospel matter as much as the content of the message itself. Christ calls us to an identity of love that demonstrates consistency between the message of the gospel and the method by which we communicate that message. His Great Commandments clearly articulate the life to which he calls us.

The Priority of the Great Commandments of Jesus

When Jesus calls his followers to love with heart, soul, mind, and strength, he calls us to let love characterize our lives "to the uttermost degree."[11] These four terms together signify the whole of the human person, as Evans comments in the *Word Biblical Commentary*:

> The three or four modifiers of the command to love the Lord God are meant to convey the totality of one's being and resources. The modifiers are not synonymous, to be sure. *Kardia*, "heart", can mean "mind" in Semitic texts. The heart is the seat of spiritual life and the inner being, among other things. *Psuche*, "life" or "soul", refers to life itself, though often with reference to feelings, emotions, and desires, and thus overlaps at points with *kardia*. *Dianoia*, "mind", refers to understanding and intelligence and in the LXX often translates "heart." *Ischus*, "strength", is roughly synonymous with *dunamis*, "might" . . . [and] refers to one's ability, or to one's capacity or power to act.[12]

In this collection of terms, we see every aspect of the human person subsumed under an identity of love. The totality of this love may also be addressed by Mark's choice of the Greek word *agape*, which usually connotes self-sacrificial love for others. It could also be argued, however, that each of the other three Greek conceptions of love is captured in the call to love with all of our being. Loving one's spouse selflessly in a sexual context (*eros*) embodies Christ's call to neighborly love in a marriage relationship. Similarly, brotherly love (*phileo*) in the way of Jesus also reflects Christ's Great Commandments. Conversely, if parents do not love their children well (*storge*), it is difficult for them to embody Christ's love in the home. When Jesus calls us to love, he calls us to submit every part of our lives and every type of relationship we have to that identity.

Jesus's choice of love as his primary command is significant. He could have chosen many other worthy commands—worship, obey, serve, know, study, honor, or think. Each of these commands appears elsewhere in Scripture, but none rises to the level of ultimacy for Christian identity. The command to love is qualitatively different from other commands, and a primary reason for this difference seems to rest in God's own character. Many theologians believe love to be God's defining characteristic. Stanley Grenz claims:

> Love is the eternal essence of the one God. But this means that Trinitarian love is not merely one attribute of God among many. Rather, love is the fundamental "attribute of God." "God is love" is the foundational ontological statement we can declare concerning the divine essence.[13]

Millard Erickson adds, "Many regard [love] as the basic attribute, the very nature or definition of God."[14] Grenz and Erickson's use of definitional words like *essence* and *nature* with regard to love are instructive. If God's defining characteristic is love, and we are made in his image, then love should define us as well.

Philosopher C. S. Evans explains this kind of definitional, essential love:

> I must distinguish love as a transitory feeling from love as a settled disposition. . . . Love in this complex, dispositional sense certainly cannot be created in a moment by an act of will, but it is the kind of thing that can be willed in the sense that a person can work at developing such a disposition.[15]

Love as settled disposition involves the whole person in ways that other commands do not. It is possible to study, serve, or obey half-heartedly. On the other hand, this kind of love necessarily incorporates all parts of a person in a voluntary commitment of one life to another and serves as a locus of spiritual identity.

Many major Christian scholars have declared the primacy of such definitional love, also emphasizing the word *essence*. Karl Barth maintains, "Love is the essence of Christian living. It is also the *conditio sine qua non*, in every conceivable connexion [*sic*]. Wherever the Christian life in commission or omission is good before God, the good thing about it is love."[16] Princeton philosopher Diogenes Allen states:

> The two great commandments are a standard by which we can measure our lives and a promise that through grace we will become people who love fully. The overriding aim of our lives is to obey God by loving God and our neighbor.[17] [He later adds:] The essence of Christian spirituality, as defined by Jesus, is loving God with all we are and all we have and loving our neighbors as ourselves.[18]

These commands do not merely call us to particular actions but to a holistic, defining identity that permeates all aspects of our lives.

While many would affirm the centrality of a love-based Christian identity, it is likely that disagreements exist about the nature of such love. Again, Christ's example shines brightly. While Christ loved the leper and the blind man through acts of compassion and generosity, he also loved Peter as he chastised him for his arrogance and the Pharisees as he called them to a true understanding of faithfulness to God. Christlike love is neither simple niceness nor mere tolerance or affirmation for another person. During his time on earth, Christ's love for people always arose from his commitment and obedience to the Father and consistently reflected the will of the Father. The love to which he calls us must be similarly rooted.

The context of Mark 12 speaks to the varied nature of such love, both in its tender compassion and its loving confrontation. In the beginning of the chapter, Jesus tells the parable of the tenants with such conviction that many Jews want to arrest him because they recognize their own sin in his story. Soon after, as the Pharisees and Sadducees try to trap him, Jesus diagnoses their hypocrisy and ignorance of God's ways and confronts them directly. Conversely, the chapter ends with Jesus affirming the generosity of the widow who gives away her only two coins. Each of these stories surrounding the declaration of the Great Commandments serves to illustrate them. Jesus communicated his love as much by correcting the errors of those who were living sinfully as he did by extending compassion to the outcasts. In his teachings and actions, Jesus showed his followers a bigger, more holistic picture of God's love that includes our affections, our understanding of truth, our sense of identity, and even our physical actions. If we want to resemble this picture, we must pursue habits that enable us to develop patterns of life that change the orientation and trajectory of the human heart.

Spiritual Disciplines for Pursuing an Identity of Love

In pursuing an identity of love, we must recognize that spiritual formation is, first of all, the work of the Holy Spirit, not a self-help project that depends on human self-discipline. One of the temptations in spiritual formation is assuming that Christ's commands, even the Great Commands, primarily require human effort. The misconception is that if believers can commit enough time and effort to the right practices, they will become more obedient, more spiritual, and closer to God. Eugene Peterson suggests that this well-intended caricature actually leads the believer away from God. He states, "Every expression of spirituality, left to itself, tends toward being more about me and less about God."[19] In other words, relying on human effort alone to be faithful to God is counterproductive.

A biblical understanding of spiritual formation, however, consistently affirms the absolute primacy of God's work and initiative in spiritual formation. In John 15, Jesus teaches about the human inability to achieve spiritual ends apart from him using the metaphor of the vine and the branches. In Romans 7, the Apostle Paul despairs at his inability to do what he knows to be good, even though in his "inner being [he] delight[s] in God's law." In John 5, Jesus declares his own reliance upon the Father, declaring his inability to do anything apart from him. While human effort is clearly required in pursuing Christlikeness, it is secondary to divine agency in the process of spiritual formation.

The role of the spiritual disciplines in spiritual formation provides a believer the opportunity to acknowledge the primacy of the Holy Spirit and to respond to the convictions that arise from it. While the disciplines in and of themselves are not transformative, faithful, intentional practice provides a Christian with "relational opportunities to open the heart to the Spirit who transforms."[20] Through such practice, the believer provides fertile ground for the Spirit to cultivate and increases his or her personal awareness of the Spirit's work. Spiritual disciplines help develop habits that shape identity over time, and these habits help us become aware of areas in our lives that stray from God's ideal and provide opportunities for us to present ourselves as willing recipients of the Holy Spirit's transforming work.

It can be helpful to regard spiritual disciplines as falling into two different categories. The first category is composed of what can be considered "classical disciplines" such as daily prayer, Bible study, and regular church involvement. These disciplines should be central to a believer's life, because they have the potential to focus one's attention on the shaping work of the Holy Spirit, especially if one is focused on the *telos* of an identity of love. The following two examples, which may be less familiar to evangelicals, illustrate how to focus our prayer and Scripture reading in ways that allow God to reshape the core of who we are—to change us at such an internal level that our normal way of acting in relationships with others is fundamentally changed. They are more than daily habits or tasks of obedience; they are instruments that God uses to conform us to the likeness of Christ.

Examen prayer comes from the Ignatian tradition and provides a believer with opportunities to review one's daily activities and attitudes for the purpose of identifying God's work in one's life. This practice sees prayer as more than just a list of requests but rather as an opportunity to pay attention to the probing work of the Holy Spirit. This practice incorporates the following five steps:

1. Become aware of God's presence.
2. Review the day with gratitude.
3. Pay attention to your emotions.
4. Choose one feature of the day and pray from it.
5. Look toward tomorrow.

Incorporating this practice into one's prayer life can be helpful in pursuing an identity of love. Daily *examen* prayer provides an opportunity for the Holy Spirit to convict, teach, and guide us as we reflect on ways that we may or may not have imitated Christ's love in our actions. For example, one may realize at the end of a particular day that he or she has acted selfishly or with irritation with a coworker. Upon such recognition, that person could ask God to help him or her act with love in very specific ways the next day. Over time, this process of awareness and action leads an individual to adopt a different standard of "normal" behavior toward the coworker—one that inherently reflects God's love. Over time, as the individual submits more and more areas of life to the work of the Holy Spirit, that person's identity gradually changes to one of a person who is characterized by love.

Another spiritual discipline that helps believers become more aware of God's voice in shaping their identity is *lectio divina* ("spiritual reading" in Latin). This ancient approach to reading Scripture shifts the responsibility for gaining insight from the reader to the Holy Spirit. Some evangelicals, because of their high regard for Scripture, take a very analytical approach to the Bible in an effort to interpret it correctly. This analytical approach, however, can often lead readers to set an agenda for Scripture, rather than allowing the Holy Spirit to speak freely in unplanned ways. *Lectio divina* emphasizes that Scripture is the living Word of God that is to be received by the believer and not just studied. The reader trusts that the Holy Spirit who inspired the words of Scripture is still at work in illuminating its meaning and application. In this process, the reader engages Scripture in the following four ways:

1. *Lectio* ("read")
2. *Meditatio* ("meditate")
3. *Oratio* ("pray")
4. *Contemplatio* ("contemplate")

When we read Scripture in this manner, we often hear elements of the text in fresh ways that speak to the core issues of our lives. Part of the reason that we are able to hear Scripture anew is that we seek to approach Scripture selflessly. We do not go to Scripture looking for specific answers but go to listen for the voice of the Holy Spirit, who may speak into any area of life from the text. Reading the Bible in this way shifts our focus from a drive to master concepts to seeing Scripture as a means for God to shape our identities. Such an approach does not negate the important work of discernment and the faithful interpretation of Scripture, but provides opportunities for the Holy Spirit to speak to us about areas of life and truth that may not be "on our radar" when we sit down to read. Shifting the locus of control away from the self in reading Scripture is not only good theology; it also helps shape us into becoming more selfless in other areas of our lives. Selflessness, of course, is essential for living a life of love.

In addition to these classic spiritual disciplines of *examen* prayer and *lectio divina*, responsive, or situational, disciplines serve to help a believer become more aware of God's voice through the normal activities of daily life. Whereas the classical disciplines emphasize intentionality, responsive disciplines, although they are not directly addressed in Scripture, arise from the recognition that spiritual formation often happens in the serendipitous moments when God intervenes in our lives. Eighteenth-century priest Jean-Pierre de Caussade called this the "sacrament of the present moment" and stated, "All that takes place within us, around us, or through us, contains and conceals His divine action."[21] God is always at work in the lives of believers, and calls us to develop the vision and awareness to recognize and respond to God's work. Responsive disciplines help the believer pay attention to the work of the Holy Spirit so that he or she is receptive to serendipity when it arrives. These disciplines help us, in particular, to respond proactively when we are paying attention to God's voice. When we are more attentive, we discover that God can use anything to change us.

In my own life, two personal anecdotes illustrate how believers can reimagine the normal activities of our lives as spiritual disciplines that God can use to conform us to the image of Christ. Several years ago, I watched a comedy movie that will never show up on anyone's list of great films. God, however, used this movie to convict me of an area of sin, and an unloving identity in my life. In the movie *Click*, the main character acquires a universal remote control that allows him to actually control the universe. He is a workaholic and his life is out of balance, so he uses the remote control to pause his family life so he can work more or fast-forward through family events so that he can get back to work faster. He discovers, of course, that he has developed a pattern of life that disconnects him from his family, and he loses what is most important to him. As I watched this movie, I felt a very strong sense of conviction from the Holy

Spirit that I was watching a fictionalized version of my own life. Through a bad comedy, God made me aware of the damaging consequences of my own tendencies toward workaholism. The movie became a catalyst for practical, daily changes in my life that have helped reshape the core of my identity. For example, seeing 5:00 P.M. on the clock on my computer is now a daily opportunity for me to choose whether I will prioritize my family or my work. Over time, as I choose my family more regularly, my identity has shifted so that prioritizing my family is becoming a normal part of my life. God speaks to all believers in similar, significant ways on a regular basis if we are willing to listen and respond.

A student's story illustrates another practical way to pay attention and then act upon God's conviction through responsive spiritual disciplines. One Tuesday I walked into chapel and noticed that a student had dyed her hair, changing it from black to almost white. When I asked her about it, she explained how she had recognized God's conviction in one area of her life. God had shown her that she was judgmental, particularly of people who changed their external appearance. She felt that one way God wanted her to address her judgmental attitude was to dye her own hair and be on the receiving end of questions and comments. When asked how it was going, she responded, "I hate it." She explained, however, how the daily routine of fixing her hair and of responding to questions about her appearance had become tools of the Holy Spirit to change her attitude toward other people. Her time in front of the mirror each day had become a spiritual discipline, a way to pay attention to the Holy Spirit's shaping work in her life. This student recognized that God wanted some significant, identity-level changes in her life, and she was willing to respond to the Spirit's convicting work by adapting her daily practices. These practices were not spiritual in and of themselves, but they became tools of the Holy Spirit to help her listen to God's voice.

If God is constantly at work around us, trying to get our attention, as seems evident, one of the most faithful things we can do is to learn how to pay attention and respond in practical ways. As we do this, we discover that our core identity becomes increasingly reflective of the life and love of Christ.

Conclusion

Christ's call is to let our love for God and others increasingly character-ize our lives. The goal of this process is not to diminish the importance of doctrine, Scripture, truth, or behavioral purity, but to ground them in an identity of love that permeates every aspect of our lives so that we more closely resemble Christ. We need this picture of Christ's model of maturity, because what we see as maturity shapes us. If we see theological faithful-ness as maturity, the scholar becomes the picture of maturity. If we see acts of service as the picture of maturity, the busy person becomes the model. Christ gave the church a more holistic picture—a person who demon-strates love for God and others in every area of life. Pursuing this picture means that the loving person becomes the model. And that is exactly what we see in the model God provided for us.

God so loved us that he sent his Son for us, and his Son so loved us that he relinquished all his rights so that we could receive God's love. He did not, however, choose love over obedience to the Father's will or a clear understanding of and commitment to the truth of God's Word. Christ never set up false dichotomies. In his interactions with sinners and Pharisees, with outcasts and disciples, he consistently held together what we tend to separate. He challenged Pharisees to recognize that disciplined study and faithfulness to the minutia of religious law did not make them obedient to God's will. At the same time, when Christ showed compassion for those caught in sin, he did not exempt them from the need for obedience and righteousness. In the case of Zacchaeus, this sinner responded to Christ's loving act of acknowledgment by recognizing his own sin and making restitution to those he had cheated (Luke 19:1–10). Similarly, Christ's acceptance of the Samaritan woman at the well enabled her to worship Christ and to offer testimony to her neighbors. In these cases, Christ's compassionate love allowed each person to recognize his or her distance from God's standard of holiness and the need for repentance. While both people were already very aware of their sinful behavior (the religious people in their communities had probably challenged them about their sin), Christ reached them in ways that others could not because his love communicated God's truth in ways that mere recitation of the law could not. By initiating relationships with people in love, he made it possible for them to recognize God's truth and respond.

When Jesus was asked to define what is most important in life with God, his response was clear. The primary identity for those who truly know God is to love God to the utmost of their being, and to love others as themselves. He modeled this love in all that he did, and our call as his followers is to have the same attitude and identity he did—an identity of love that selflessly gives itself away in obedience to the Father.

NOTES

[1] Some examples include the Good Samaritan, the little children coming to Jesus, and many of the stories of his interactions with the Pharisees.

[2] Richard E. Averbeck, "The Bible in Spiritual Formation," in *The Kingdom Life: A Practical Theology of Discipleship and Spiritual Formation*, ed. Alan Andrews (Colorado Springs, CO: NavPress, 2010), 299.

[3] C. Stephen Evans, "Is There a Basis for Loving All People?," *Journal of Psychology and Theology* 34, no. 1 (2001): 84.

[4] David W. Bebbington, *The Dominance of Evangelicalism* (Oxford: Oxford University Press, 2005), 21–40. Parenthetical comments are the author's.

[5] David Kinnaman and Gabe Lyons, *UnChristian: What a New Generation Really Thinks about Christianity and Why It Matters* (Grand Rapids, MI: Baker Books, 2007), 24–30.

[6] James K. A. Smith, *You Are What You Love: The Spiritual Power of Habit* (Grand Rapids, MI: Brazos Press, 2016), 2.

[7] St. Augustine, *On Christian Doctrine* (Mineola, NY: Dover Philosophical Classics, 2009), 24.

[8] Dallas Willard, *Renovation of the Heart: Putting on the Character of Christ* (Colorado Springs, CO: NavPress, 2002), 39.

[9] Thomas Aquinas, *Nature and Grace: Selections from the Summa Theologica of Thomas Aquinas*, ed. and trans. A. M. Fairweather, Library of Christian Classics, vol. 11 (London: SCM Press, 1954), 140–56.

[10] Alister E. McGrath, *Mere Apologetics: How to Help Seekers and Skeptics Find Faith* (Grand Rapids, MI: Baker Books, 2012), 16.

[11] Alexander B. Bruce, "The Synoptic Gospels," in *The Expositor's Greek Testament*, ed. W. Robertson Nicoll (Grand Rapids, MI: Eerdmans, 1956), 424.

[12] Evans, "Is There a Basis," 264.

[13] Stanley J. Grenz, *Theology for the Community of God* (Nashville: Broadman & Holman, 1994), 72.

[14] Millard J. Erickson, *Christian Theology*, 2nd ed. (Grand Rapids, MI: Baker Books, 1998), 318. See also 1 John 4 and 2 Corinthians 13.

[15] Evans, "Is There a Basis," 81.

[16] Karl Barth, *Church Dogmatics*, vol. 1 (Edinburgh: T&T Clark, 1956), 372.

[17] Diogenes Allen, *Spiritual Theology: The Theology of Yesterday for Spiritual Help Today* (Cambridge, MA: Cowley Publications, 1997), 24.

[18] Barry D. Jones, "Book Symposium: Spiritual Formation as If the Church Mattered," *Journal of Spiritual Formation and Soul Care* 1, no. 2 (2008): 245.

[19] Eugene Peterson, "Spirituality for All the Wrong Reasons," *Christianity Today* 49, no. 3 (2005): 47.

[20] John Coe, "Resisting the Temptation of Moral Formation: Opening to Spiritual Formation in the Cross and the Spirit," *Journal of Spiritual Formation and Soul Care* 1, no. 1 (2008): 66.

[21] Jean-Pierre de Caussade, *Abandonment to Divine Providence*, trans. E. J. Strickland (St. Louis: B. Herder, 1921), 3.

An Identity of Forgiveness in Colossians
A New Way of Being

CÉLESTIN MUSEKURA

Therefore, as God's chosen people, holy and dearly loved, clothe
yourselves with compassion, kindness, humility, gentleness and
patience. Bear with each other, and forgive one another if any of you
has a grievance against someone. Forgive as the Lord forgave you.

—Colossians 3:12–13

In my nearly twenty-five years of ministry with African Leadership and Reconciliation Ministries (ALARM), I have had the opportunity to invite thousands of pastors and community leaders to walk the path of forgiveness. In pursuing forgiveness, we are like toddlers, stumbling in our shaky attempts to live a new life in Christ. As we keep our eyes fixed on Jesus, however, we are elevated above our own abilities and are

Adapted material from *Forgiving as We've Been Forgiven*, by L. Gregory Jones and Célestin Musekura. Copyright © 2010 by L. Gregory Jones and Célestin Musekura. Used by permission of InterVarsity Press, P.O. Box 1400, Downers Grove, IL 60515. http://www.ivpress.com.

transformed by the one who has forgiven us into people who can also forgive. Whether within the context of a broken family, a divided church, or a nation at war, peace is never the achievement of those with exceptional skill or untiring commitment. Forgiveness is always a gift, and it is rarely earned. Like a new suit of clothes, forgiveness covers our shame and dresses us up for the heavenly banquet. When God clothes us in forgiveness, we may be so overwhelmed by the experience of a restored relationship with our creator that we forget an equally important truth: our new outfit changes what we look like to other people. With a transformed appearance, we become new people when we "put on" Christ.

In Colossians 3:1–17, the apostle Paul reminds us that identification with Christ through his death and resurrection seals our new identity. With this new identity, our thoughts, minds, aspirations, and conduct rise to a new level that requires us to renounce behaviors that divide, disrupt, and cause tension with others. In imitation of Christ, believers must build up the community by exercising virtues such as sympathy, kindness, humility, meekness, and patience. Although these virtues guard against conflicts and quarrels, we never master them, and they do not guarantee painless relationships. Forgiveness, then, is a craft we learn to practice in concert with these virtues as we seek unity and peace in the community where the Word of God is lived out and God is worshiped.

Our new identity as a forgiven people who practice forgiveness requires a renewal of our humanity and a recognition of God's image in others—even those we have considered our enemies. This new perspective does not happen automatically. In social spaces that are fragmented by injustice, tribal/ethnic violence, racial discrimination, gender oppression, marital infidelity, failed expectations, and disappointment, granting and receiving forgiveness is difficult. After listening to many stories of deep brokenness, I've come to name three wounds that need to be healed in each of our lives: wounds of the heart, wounds of the mind, and wounds that arise from patterns of unjust action against ourselves and others.

As psychologists and social workers often remind us, abusers are almost always victims before they become perpetrators. In a world twisted by sin, our hearts are broken before they harden. After we have been hurt emotionally, our minds begin to think and plan vengeance, and we begin to act in a harmful manner not only toward those who have caused us pain, but also toward ourselves and even those we love. Until our hearts and minds are renewed by forgiveness, our actions perpetuate this cycle of hatred, vengeance, and self-destruction. Drawing from my own ministry experiences in Africa, I will define forgiveness and describe, based on Colossians 3:12–13, what living with a new heart, mind, and behavior looks like.

Forgiveness

Forgiveness is usually defined as a behavior, a disposition, and a process.[1] In this way, forgiveness is a way of being, an identity that one adopts. Adopting an identity of forgiveness begins a process of reconciliation that is the "quieter revolution"—a daily transformation of being that breathes life into a broken world.[2] Many theories and definitions have been posited by psychologists and theologians about the nature of forgiveness, but I have come to the conclusion that forgiveness is "to release or to set one free from a debt while dismissing any charge against" another person.[3] Neil Anderson goes even further to describe forgiveness as "agreeing to live with the consequences of another person's sin."[4]

What I have witnessed in my own life and in the lives of countless others is the good news that God can heal hearts, minds, and actions through the practice of forgiveness. I am convinced that this holistic renewal of the individual and his or her community is at the heart of Jesus's message and the primary work of the church in the world. When we witness both the healing of old wounds and the possibility of new relationships through forgiveness, we learn what it means to "put on Christ." Forgiveness, however, is painful and expensive; it requires a radical shift of one's self-understanding, along with a new heart, a new mind, and a new way of living.

A New Heart

Though I have heard countless people say that their hearts are sick because of the evil that has been done to them, it is anger, bitterness, and resentment that truly sicken the heart. Others have confessed that their bitterness has caused both emotional turmoil and disrupted relationships with innocent spouses, children, relatives, and neighbors. A troubled heart makes unforgiving people double victims—victims of both their offenders and of their own hatred. In my numerous visits to Africa, speaking at conferences on forgiveness and reconciliation between different African tribes, I have met many people—even pastors and church leaders—with sickened hearts. I also have seen how sincere forgiveness can liberate a heart and bring it back to a life of purpose, able to joyfully serve the community.

I witnessed one particularly memorable transformation during a conference on forgiveness at the Agricultural University in Gulu, Uganda. During the conference, Pastor Okoch from Gulu shared his personal story of unforgiveness with more than a hundred pastors and church leaders after his heart had been renewed by the proceedings. Years of war in northern Uganda have produced not only what has been called the "invisible children"—orphans drafted into the armies of their parents' killers—but also countless widows, widowers, and childless parents who have suffered the brutality of government soldiers and rebel forces, especially from Joseph Kony's Lord's Resistance Army (LRA). Pastor Okoch was only eight years old when he watched government soldiers hang and kill his father, who was accused of siding with the LRA rebels, in the city market of Gulu. In the years that followed, Okoch grew up with hatred and bitterness in his heart, looking for ways to avenge his father and the other Acholi tribesmen who were killed by these soldiers of the government of Yoweli Museveni. Okoch was angry at not only the government but also the other tribes that had supported the government. Even after he became a pastor of one of the churches in northern Uganda, he continued to resent anything the government did, good or bad. For him, all those in government—the president, members of the cabinet, leaders in the government party, members of the Ugandan army and police, and any tribe that collaborated with them—were thieves and murderers.

By the time I met him, twenty-seven years of hatred and resentment had hardened Pastor Okoch and affected the people around him, including members of his church. At the conference he admitted to me, "For the last eight years as a pastor, I have never preached on forgiveness because I did not want to forgive anyone. There are people in my congregation that I hate because they belong to what I consider the wrong people, the wrong tribe, and wrong political party." The shameful death of his father and the oppression of his tribe had turned his heart black and hard. Okoch's wounded, hardened heart was full of poison, and everything that came out of him was poisonous to his family and community. Okoch became a victim of his own hatred, and he did not have someone to show him the way of peace and forgiveness. Okoch's hatred, as of late, had taken an even darker turn. In fact, to the surprise of all the conference participants, Okoch confessed that his hatred for the government of Museveni had turned him into a dangerous person, as he had started asking God to side with him against those he hated. Pastor Okoch admitted that he had been praying for "demons" to "possess the government and the president of Uganda."

I remember vividly how I felt in that classroom at the Agriculture University. Pastor Okoch's hatred was palpable, and I began to wonder what I had said to compel this man to stand up and share all these dark secrets. My ALARM colleagues, Nelson and Jessica, looked at me in amazement, and I wondered if I should ask the pastor to end his testimony or allow him to continue. A silence that I rarely experience with African pastors and lay leaders filled the room.

A transformation, one that could only have been orchestrated by God, took place. By this time Pastor Okoch trembled, and tears flowed from his eyes. He used his tie to wipe tears from his cheeks. A number of participants wept with him; it was obvious that they had joined Pastor Okoch on his journey toward a renewed and healed heart. In that room I saw a fellowship of the wounded, but I also sensed that God was doing something new for this community—a community of believers from different tribes who had been enemies for a long time. Hebrews 12:14–15 states, "Pursue peace with everyone. . . . See to it that no one fails to obtain the grace of God; that no root of bitterness springs up and causes trouble, and through it many become defiled" (NASB). God, in his grace, had given Pastor Okoch a new vision and a new heart. This man had realized for the first time in twenty-seven years that he could be set free, his heart and mind renewed.

As he continued to narrate his story, Pastor Okoch looked around the room and began calling the names of other pastors who were present, asking them to forgive him because he had hated them. He confessed that he was one of those who had worked to dismantle the Gulu Pastors Fellowship because he did not want to associate with pastors and church leaders from other tribes and other regions of Uganda. Pastor Okoch repented of his hatred to everyone, including the government of Uganda. He promised that on the following Sunday (two days later) he would ask his congregation to forgive him for being a bitter, hateful, and vengeful pastor. He asked for prayers that God, who had renewed his heart, would continue to renew his mind so he might bear the fruit of peace and love to all people.

After Pastor Okoch spoke, a few men and women stood up to offer forgiveness to our repentant brother and apologize for the sins of their own kinsmen during the ethnic violence that divided Uganda. Still many more identified with not only his woundedness but also his anger. Pastor Okoch's honesty helped them—and me—to see how desperately we need to put on Christ. Thankfully, God's forgiveness is a salve for our wounds and heals us in ways that we cannot imagine. Like a good doctor, God often interrupts us when we least want treatment, reaching through our tears and resistance to disturb old wounds. Whether we know it or not, this is the beginning of a holistic transformation. When God wants to clothe us with the virtues of holiness, he begins by touching our broken hearts.

A New Mind

Paul reminds the Colossians that because of their new identity in Christ, their thoughts must be renewed and refocused. Instead of focusing on earthly things, they must set their minds on heavenly matters by replacing carnal thinking with a renewed knowledge of Christ through whom people of every tribe, race, and socioeconomic status are forgiven and reconciled (Col. 3:10–11). For Paul, a renewed mind gives actions their meaning. He instructs believers in Rome, Ephesus, and Colossae to have their minds renewed so that they may know and understand God's will for their daily lives and Christian witness (Rom. 12:2; Eph. 4:23; Col. 1:9; 3:2). As David Garland puts it: "Christians should not shy away from the fact that our lives are centered on the divine things. We offer a different way of making sense of reality and a different way of living, which go against the grain of what modern society offers as the norm."[5]

It is not enough for God to touch and heal our hearts, because our minds nurse grudges and relive the pain and injuries caused to us. Our minds poison us with reasons why a person, tribe, race, or some sin, offense, or hurt should never be forgiven. In our minds, we condemn others without giving them the chance to clarify or defend themselves, acknowledge their guilt, or repent. Almost everything we put into action has been planned and executed in our minds. This is why the renewal of our mind is critical for altering our actions.

Transformation begins with a renewed mind, and Paul advises the Roman believers that a renewed mind is the antidote for worldliness. "Do not be conformed to this world," he tells them, "but be transformed by the renewal of your mind, that by testing you may discern what is the will of God, what is good and acceptable and perfect" (Rom. 12:2 ESV). Anger, resentment, and unforgiveness corrode the mind. When our relationships have been injured by people who are close to us, our minds quickly forget the good and beautiful days we have had with them and fixate only on the wrong they have done. Soon we begin to plan how we might avoid them or even how to get even. Our minds give us reasons and justification for our own evil plans while blinding us to the role we have played in a broken relationship. Our minds ease us into blaming, judging, and even seeking revenge. Christians play along with this vicious cycle by responding to injuries, conflicts, and violence with a conscious forgetfulness of the desire of God for us to be kind to one another and forgive one another as God in Christ has forgiven us (Eph. 4:32).

A good illustration of this kind of transformation and forgiveness is the story of Clementine. When I first met Clementine on one of my visits to Goma in the Democratic Republic of Congo, she washed my hands and served me a meal. She had told an ALARM staff member that she wanted to serve and care for the man of God who had founded the organization that had brought her "to the right mind." I did not know Clementine's story until the following day when my colleagues told me how ALARM's teaching on biblical forgiveness was impacting Congolese families and communities that were suffering in eastern Congo. They also told me that Clementine would be graduating that day from ALARM's Pastoral Leadership Training Institute (PLTI), a three-year program that trains key leaders to carry on our work of reconciliation in Africa.

Years before, Clementine's heart had been hardened by a family betrayal. She was born out of wedlock to a young teenager and was raised by her grandmother. Because of the shame, guilt, and stigma associated with teen pregnancies and children born from such taboo relationships, Clementine had been "protected" from this information by family deceptions. She eventually learned the truth, however, in a painful episode that one day before her wedding left a big scar on her heart and sealed her mind in hatred and resentment of both her real grandmother (whom she knew as her "mother") and her biological mother (whom she knew as her "sister").

According to tradition, on the day before Clementine's wedding, gifts were given to the family of the bride. One special gift was designated for the bride's mother, and to Clementine's amazement and shame, the person she knew as a sister went forward to receive it. It was at that moment that Clementine learned the truth that her mother was, in fact, her grandmother, and the sister with whom she had shared laughter, tears, and life secrets was actually her mother. From that moment until almost thirteen years later, Clementine did not speak to her family. She hated them, and in her mind, she considered them dead.

As the years passed, Clementine could not think of anything except the wrong done to her. She later testified that she could never think of anything good, anything beautiful, or anything worthwhile about her "mother-grandmother," her "sister-mother," or other members of her family. She even took no joy in her own husband and children, because her mind could not allow her heart to feel love for them.

Clementine's mind was renewed, however, when she understood the cost of her own forgiveness from God and God's command to forgive others in the same way. She was ministered to by one of my colleagues, Marie-Jeanne, and ten other influential Congolese women who had attended my training on biblical forgiveness and reconciliation in Kigali. Upon their return to Goma, they had organized their own conference, which Clementine had attended.

Clementine learned about God's forgiveness at the conference, along with Marie-Jeanne's personal testimony of how she forgave the stepmother who had tied her hands together and doused them in kerosene, ready to set them on fire as punishment for her alleged theft of a slice of bread. Clementine realized that she also could free her mind of toxic thoughts by letting go of her resentment against her family. She felt God's conviction that unless her mind was renewed and her heart delivered, she would continue to hurt her husband and ten children. Clementine then gathered the courage to ask the women at the conference to pray for her broken heart and renewal of mind. From that moment on, Clementine began a journey toward restoration, finding those who had hurt her in order to forgive them and love them again.

New Actions

As hearts are healed and minds are restored through forgiveness, the result is new attitudes and behaviors that build up communities. When Paul exhorts believers to be compassionate, humble, patient, kind, tolerant, and forgiving in Colossians 3:12, he reminds them that this way of life will set them apart from others around them. Because members of the church come from different ethnic, social, and cultural groups, the possibility of tension always exists. While Clementine and some members of her family had been church members before her encounter with the practice of forgiveness, disappointment and shame had caused their physical and emotional separation. Like many nominal Christians today in many churches, they sang of the grace of God but were never touched and transformed by it. They knew something was not right in their relationships, but they did not know how to address the problem, and their pastors were not able to help them. They lived as enemies even though they professed to belong to the source of reconciliation. They sang about God's forgiveness of sins, but they failed to grant the same forgiveness to each other. Both their attitudes and their actions were impaired by their history.

By the time I met Clementine, she had already found her mother, grandmother, and other relatives and forgiven them. On the day of her graduation from our Pastoral Leadership Training Institute, Clementine's husband told me that God, through ALARM'S teaching of forgiveness, had given him a new wife with a new heart and a new mind. Their marriage of fifteen years has had peace and tranquility since Clementine experienced the power of forgiveness.

Today, Clementine's life is full of thanksgiving to God for his redeeming love and for the restoration of broken relationships through forgiveness. My brief conversation with Clementine on the second day of our encounter did not reveal any signs of hatred or misery. She had a radiant face, a beautiful, shy smile, and the elegant look of someone with a clear purpose. Her husband told me that she is now gentle, patient, humble, kind, and generous. Another staff member said her actions toward her family members have inspired women in the village and in the church to also pursue forgiveness. Clementine has been involved in serving with ALARM ministries to internally displaced peoples (IDPs) around Goma. Service, for her, has become a way of life. Clementine's new actions are characterized by a heart full of joy and thanksgiving for the provision that God has made through the acts of receiving and granting the gift of forgiveness. During our lunch together, I counted it a great honor and privilege to be physically fed by someone who had been spiritually fed by my fellow servants in eastern Congo.

Like Clementine, a new mind led Pastor Okoch to new actions. After his speech at the conference, he promised to go back to his church to ask for the forgiveness of his congregation and also promised that he would work with other church leaders to revive the Gulu Pastors Fellowship. A few weeks later, we learned that more than eighteen pastors from six different denominations in the war-torn city of Gulu had joined the fellowship; they were meeting in each other's homes, sharing food, and planning an evangelistic crusade together. They began to teach and preach forgiveness and reconciliation. Through this fellowship, ALARM began to partner with these pastors to identify widows and orphans who needed assistance. Today there are more than 350 orphans of war who are being educated through the partnership of ALARM, the churches in northern Uganda, and partner churches in the United States.

However, forgiveness and reconciliation must also take place beyond the church, between former tribal enemies. ALARM brings widows together from warring tribes and teaches these women mutual understanding and that their futures are bound together. By working together in a business, they learn to trust each other, to support each other, and to depend on each other. These women are discipled together, and they pray together for their children and their businesses. They are hoping together, and they are building a new community that is committed to raising up their children in the spirit of forgiveness, nonviolence, and mutual acceptance.

Fostering Forgiveness as a Community

When Paul instructs and commands Colossians to put to death sins of desire such as immorality, impurity, lust, evil desires, and greed (Col. 3:5), and to get rid of sins like anger, rage, malice, slander, filthy language, and lies (Col. 3:8–9), he is aware that these vices destroy communities. When our hearts and minds are wounded, we inevitably hurt the people around us, causing them to put up walls of defensiveness. Sin not only hurts the sinner; it destroys human community. David Garland summarizes the effects of the sins of anger in a community more vividly:

> Anger refers to a chronic feeling as opposed to outburst of rage. More subtle expressions of anger ooze out in the malice we bear others and the spiteful potshots we take to defame their reputations. Filthy language from your lips does not simply refer to curse words. It has in mind the abusive language we use to hurt others. Christian speech is not determined solely by whether it is true or false but by whether it helps or harms another. . . . Putting off falsehood and speaking the truth are linked to all being "members of one body," and lying is rooted in an attempt to gain advantage over others. It therefore is at odds with Christian love even though Christians have been known to concoct lies to deceive others (see Acts 5:1–11). Such deceit reveals a lack of mutual trust, undermines community, and breeds anger.[6]

For both Pastor Okoch and Clementine, anger began the process that led to hatred, resentment, and unforgiveness. When a community of believers harbors anger, a root of bitterness is planted—one that threatens to defile many. Okoch and Clementine were not the only ones affected by their unforgiveness and resentment; their relatives, family members, church members, and communities were also defiled. Through the understanding and the practice of biblical forgiveness, these two saints are reversing the effect of unforgiveness in their lives and communities. Christ is not only being honored in their lives; he is also being glorified in their families and communities. These two have been beneficiaries of their own gracious gift of forgiveness to those who have hurt and caused pain and sorrow in their lives. But many others, including myself, have also benefited from their courageous act of forgiveness. Both Okoch and Clementine forgave their debtors from their hearts, and their forgiveness was authenticated by new actions.

Forgiveness from the heart is a supernatural act. When we are wrongly hurt or injured, our wounded hearts can instruct us to harbor grudges and seek revenge in the name of justice, even if we are Christians. Or, when we do forgive, but this forgiveness is motivated by mere human kindness and goodness, it is most of the time shallow and superficial, or a way to postpone revenge and punishment. It may be also a social mechanism used to distance the forgiven from the forgiver. This human forgiveness may be the killer of Christian fellowship or any communion.

Mere human forgiveness comes from the lips, not from the heart. Jesus warned his disciples about this kind of "Pharisaic" forgiveness and instructed his followers that true forgiveness must be conceived in the memory of our own forgiveness. It must be granted from the heart and must be expressed in practical actions as the forgiver releases the debtors and welcomes them back into fellowship and friendship (Matt. 18:23–35). This supernatural forgiveness can seem impossible for men and women who, like Peter, ask the question: "how many times should I forgive someone who keeps sinning against me?" (Matt. 18:21). Indefinitely, Jesus answered. Without Christ, who could possibly forgive the crimes of murder, kidnapping, theft, or deceit?

Colossians 3: 1–17 clearly confirms that when our tribal, racial, social, and economic identity is renewed by surrendering ourselves to Christ, our hearts and minds engage in actions that are supernatural. Putting on Christ enables believers to keep on forgiving their parents, spouses, children, neighbors, and even the murderers of one's family members and friends.

Christ in us makes this forgiveness possible because our hearts and minds have been renewed for divinely enabled actions. We can live a life that is pleasing to God when we take on the identity of Christ, and those who are being renewed in the image of Christ are enabled to produce Christlike conduct because their new nature dictates it. They will not do so completely and perfectly, but their minds and intentions are divinely inspired. When they realized that they could forgive their tormentors and enemies, Clementine and Okoch discovered this secret.

Bitterness and hatred spares no one. I myself have had to forgive those who have done me great harm—something I could not have done without the supernatural aid of Jesus. One such person was Jean Batiste (John the Baptizer), a Rwandan pastor whose family members were murdered in 1990 when the then Uganda-based Tutsi rebels of the Rwanda Patriotic Front (RPF) attacked Rwanda, an event that later led to the Rwandan genocide of 1994. Jean escaped the massacres in his village in the northern region of Byumba and became a displaced person. He lived in a camp of IDPs in Rwanda for four years. Jean's anger and bitterness against the rebels and most Tutsis increased in his heart as the war between the Tutsi rebels and Hutu-dominated Rwandan army raged on in different parts of the country. Jean and other survivors of the massacres in his village moved from one IDP camp to another, finally ending up in a refugee camp near Goma, in eastern Democratic Republic of Congo. Lost in his anger and vengeful thoughts, Jean forgot his identity in Christ and chose instead to embrace his tribal identity, which motivated him to hate, fight, and seek revenge. His heart, mind, and actions were submitted to the will and desire of his inner demons and caused him to even praise those who killed "cockroaches," a dehumanizing term for the Tutsis by the Interahamwe militia and other Hutu extremists.[7]

When I met Jean in the Mugunga refugee camp in 1994, he was full of bitterness and hatred not only for Tutsis but also for people like me: Hutus who spoke about forgiveness and reconciliation between the two warring tribes. Because of the ministry work I was doing in Goma, Jean became my sworn enemy and convinced the Hutu militia in the Mugunga refugee camp that I was working for the Tutsi government in Rwanda. While Jean never attacked me himself, he encouraged those who lured me away from the main camp to a eucalyptus forest, where they tortured and beat me. Jean later died of cholera in the Mugunga refugee camps, and I was told that he died unhappy and vengeful—a miserable pastor. I mourned the death of my brother Jean, since, with Jesus's help, I found peace with him and forgave him even before his death.

Putting to death all vices that destroy community and putting on Christ will enable Christians to become agents of forgiveness who build communities of forgiveness and hope in places of brokenness. Genocide against Tutsis and moderate Hutus in my home country of Rwanda, the massacres of Burundian Hutus by Tutsi, the killings of innocent Congolese people by both Hutu militia and vengeful Tutsi soldiers and rebels, massacres of Tutsi Banyamulenge by militia Hutu and Mai Mai rebels, the massacres of black Christians and animists in southern Sudan by the Khartoum government, the genocide of black Darfurians by Arab Janjaweed and the Arab-dominated government of Khartoum, massacres of northern Ugandans by both government soldiers and rebels of the Lord's Resistance Army, killings of more than twelve hundred Kenyans by brutal tribal clashes and policemen—all of these heinous acts in our time call the Christian community to examine its message of forgiveness in a world full of anger and revenge. Could it be that what the world most needs today is communities that embody forgiveness? How might we produce more Clementines and Okoches? How do we help the Jean Batistes whose pain, anger, and vengeance have turned them into what they first hated?

Concluding Remarks

The message of forgiveness is needed now more than ever before. For all the categories that are used to separate people (by tribe, race, class, culture, faith, or place), forgiveness is the means by which we bridge those disputes and heal.[8] Christians need to adopt an identity of forgiveness through Christ in order to bring hope and healing to those who are hurting. I am glad that I have already enlisted in this cause and will continue to call others to their proper identity in Christ. In our world of divisiveness and strife, "putting on Christ" means wearing the uniform of forgiveness and fighting for the hearts and lives of broken people who are, whatever their background, never beyond reach.

NOTES

[1] Célestin Musekura, *An Assessment of Contemporary Models of Forgiveness* (New York: Peter Lang, 2010), 15.

[2] Emmanuel Katongole and Chris Rice, *Reconciling All Things: A Christian Vision for Justice, Peace and Healing* (Downers Grove, IL: InterVarsity Press, 2008), 44–45.

[3] Musekura, *Assessment*, 31.

[4] Neil T. Anderson, *The Bondage Breaker* (Eugene, OR: Harvest House Publishers, 1993), 196.

[5] David E. Garland, *The NIV Application Commentary* (Grand Rapids, MI: Zondervan, 1998), 215.

[6] Garland, *The NIV Application Commentary*, 205–6.

[7] A Kinyarwanda word, *Interahamwe* literally means those who do things together, those who work together, those who attack together, or those with one purpose. The noun comes from two words: The first is the verb "gutera," which can be translated as "to step in, to aim at" or "to attack." The second is "hamwe," which means "together" or "in oneness of purpose." This word historically could mean any group (cooperative, farmers, shepherd, and businesspeople) working together to achieve something for mutual support and unity of purpose. After the introduction of a multiparty system, most of the parties formed some youth movement. The ruling party, Mouvement Revolutionaire National pour le Développement (MRND), named theirs *Interahamwe*. As a group of mainly youth with Hutu ideologies, who were mainly uneducated and unemployed, the Interahamwe became the killing machine of Tutsis, moderate Hutus, and any others sympathetic to Tutsis during the genocide. They became, in the stories of Rwanda genocide, "Those who attack together." It is this group that tortured me in both the Congo and Tanzania refugee camps because they believed the message of repentance and reconciliation was Tutsi propaganda. Any Hutu who talked or preached about repentance and reconciliation instead of revenge and fighting for the Hutu cause was considered a traitor or a spy for the Tutsi government.

[8] Musekura, *Assessment*, 32.

Communal Perseverance in Hebrews
Christian Identity as God's Family

MARC-ANDRÉ CARON

A S a young pastor, I once sat with a woman in her midfifties who had made a profession of faith in Jesus fifteen years earlier. She explained to me why she did not need to go to church. She felt that she benefited more from "spiritual" conversations with her one Christian friend than from listening to a sermon. She felt that she did not have anything to contribute to the local body. Church was a waste of her time—the thought of sitting down for two hours was painful. My friend's complaints were not wholly untrue. Some churches do feel like a waste of time; they are filled with teaching that does not connect the Word of God to the challenges of life, "customers" that get in and get out, or—worst of all—petty and spiteful people. While she presented her position as a rational argument against church attendance, I suspected that her reluctance to submit to the Scriptures was largely fueled by past emotional hurts. As I listened to my friend's story, I thought about the classic biblical proof text for such a situation: "Not forsaking our own assembling together, as is the habit of some" (Heb. 10:25a).

This chapter will respond to my friend's challenge by examining how her criticism can be addressed by local churches while also showing that "going to church" is essential to our identities as Christians. To do so will require more than proof texting. Instead, I will examine the logic of the early Christian "sermon" known as the Epistle to the Hebrews.

While Hebrews is sometimes regarded as an opaque theological discourse, it is better understood as a sermon that was written to encourage its addressees, a persecuted community that lived in fear of death and religious persecution.[1] Its theological arguments all underscore a common behavioral goal: perseverance in faith and communal solidarity. This chapter will look at how the dissuading effects of persecution on the community can be overcome by its self-identity as God's family. The theological understanding of identity—as a child of God, as a sibling of Jesus, and as a member of a spiritual family—fosters perseverance and communal solidarity in the face of persecution. This chapter will conceptualize how persecution, which is supposed to deter one's faith, can lose its edge when one's self-identity is transformed in this manner. After examining a few concepts from the sociology of knowledge, the context in which Hebrews was written will be discussed. Then I will describe how the precarious state of this community was counterbalanced by its identity as the family of God. Finally, I will suggest how the theology of Hebrews regarding the family of God can be used to respond to the issues raised by my friend.

Methodology: A Sociology of Knowledge Approach

Sociologists Peter L. Berger and Thomas Luckmann offer a way to describe the determining effect of beliefs on behavior.[2] They argue that "reality is socially constructed, and that the sociology of knowledge must analyze the processes in which this occurs." Reality is defined as "the quality appertaining to phenomena that we recognize as having a being independent of our own volition (we cannot 'wish them away')," and they define knowledge as "the certainty that phenomena are real and that they possess specific characteristics."[3] The reality is that Mr. Smith exists, but whether Mr. Smith has a free will or has his fate sealed is socially constructed "knowledge." In other words, knowledge is the shared explanation for "the way things are"[4] held by a group. Knowledge and its accompanying ethics (e.g., norms) are passed through socialization: the dialectical process in which the individual learns what he ought and ought not do, as well as the process through which society offers feedback for his actions.

Further supporting the social order is the process of legitimation, by which is meant a "socially objectivated 'knowledge' that serves to explain and justify the social order."[5] Legitimations, then, are responses to inquiries regarding why things are institutionally arranged as they are. They do not explain what ought to be, but rather what is. Religious discourses are particularly powerful legitimations, because they ground the circumstantial in the universal, "an ultimately valid ontological status."[6] Legitimations occur in proverbs, maxims, wisdom, religious teaching, scientific discourses, and elaborate theories. In most parts of the world, for example, marrying one's own sibling is repugnant because "everyone knows" this is not right.

The most comprehensive level of legitimation comes from what Berger and Luckmann have called *symbolic universes*, which they define as "sheltering canopies over institutional order as well as over individual biography."[7] If theology, therefore, is a canopy that overshadows the life of its believers, then theology provides a context in which one's life experience is understood.

A given symbolic universe (or knowledge) requires a social base "for its continuing existence as a world that is real to actual human beings."[8] This is what Berger calls a *plausibility structure*. It is the prerequisite that applies both to legitimations and to the worlds that are legitimated, whether they are religious or not. In the case of Greco-Roman society and its Hellenistic-Jewish enclaves, the entire society served as the plausibility structure for its perspective, and all the important social processes within the first-century world served to "confirm and reconfirm the reality of [their] world."[9] Thus, persecution and social pressures can be conceived as means of socialization used by the wider Greco-Roman culture to persuade the community of believers in Hebrews to align with its own knowledge of reality.

The theology of Hebrews, as a canopy that overshadows the experience of persecution, can strengthen the plausibility structure of the church by offering a different interpretation of persecution supported by a coherent symbolic universe and by reinforcing the need to band together as a family. This holds together in the plausibility structure of the assembly (Heb. 10:25, ἐπισυναγωγή, *episynagōgē*) of the Christian family (ἀδελφότης, *adelphotēs*; Heb. 2:10; 3:1; 13:1). It is within the church that Christians receive validation and are reinforced in their beliefs, despite what the majority group presses upon them through negative signals such as persecution. Thus the community of Hebrews functioned as what Berger calls a "cognitive minority" within its larger society—that is, "a group formed around a body of deviant 'knowledge.'" In contrast, Berger asserts that "the plausibility of 'knowledge' that is not socially shared, that is challenged by our fellow men, is imperiled, not just in our dealing with others, but much more importantly in our own minds. . . . At best, a minority viewpoint is forced to be defensive. At worst, it ceases to be plausible to anyone."[10] Thus, when the author of Hebrews develops his theological arguments, he is not indulging in mere otherworldly discourse. He is developing a symbolic universe that allows his hearers to understand their own identity as children of God. This, in turn, fosters perseverance in faith and communal solidarity.

Persecution in the Book of Hebrews

Hebrews was addressed to a persecuted community that lived in the fear of suffering and death because of its religion.[11] Koester proposes that the history of the audience displays three phases: (1) proclamation and conversion, (2) persecution and solidarity, and (3) friction and malaise.[12] In the first phase, evangelists preached the gospel to the recipients, which was accompanied by miracles (2:4; 13:7). The hearers were enlightened at conversion (6:4; 10:32). Shortly thereafter, they were persecuted because of their newfound faith with physical sufferings, public shame, the confiscation of their belongings, and imprisonment (10:32–34; 13:3). They persevered, however, and displayed great solidarity. During the third phase (when they received the letter), some time had passed, and their initial convictions had started to weaken. Enough time had passed since their conversion that they could have become teachers in the interim (5:12). Their former leaders were deceased, perhaps even martyred (13:7). Their initial zeal had transformed into spiritual sluggishness (5:11; 6:12), evidenced by their inability to understand important Christological truths (5:11–14), by their decreased interest in "gathering together" (10:25), and by the diminishing intensity of their service for one another (10:24–25). The "warning passages" as a whole (2:1–4; 3:7–4:13; 5:11–6:12; 10:19–39; 12:14–29) give us a picture of a community on the verge of letting go of its confession of faith and of reverting back to its former religious commitments.

The Ethics of Hebrews and the Communal Identity of Its Recipients

Hebrews 10:25 reveals that the community of Hebrews gathered frequently. These gatherings —their plausibility structure— were the means to reinforce the socially deviant knowledge of early Christians. What happened in these meetings that worked toward this effect? First, we will look at group designations and their significance for establishing the necessary pattern of relationships between the members of the community. Second, we will consider the ethical ramifications of these newly formed familial relationships.

Self-Perception and Group Designations in Hebrews

Cultural opinions of the time period when Hebrews was written certainly influenced individuals' self-understanding and personal identity, as did the minority views of the Messianic Jewish and Christian community. The writer of Hebrews describes them as siblings in the family of God, as the migrant camp of the people of God, and emphasizes how important a group identity was for communal solidarity.

Brothers and sisters in the family of God. Although the modern West considers independence from one's family a virtue, kinship was the foundation of ancient Mediterranean culture. Families were the center of social interaction and the locus of personal meaning and worth in the community.[13] Personal sense of self-worth (e.g., honor/shame) was related to one's family's social standing. Honor was paid to parents by their children because they had given them life. One's identity was inextricably linked to family, and identification with one's family was near total. Unquestioning obedience to family authorities was expected. With regard to siblings, deSilva summarizes, "[T]he relationship between siblings is the closest, strongest and most intimate of relationships in the ancient world."[14] Solidarity and cooperation, rather than competition, were the desired traits of sibling relationships. Plutarch put forward the principle that the brother in a superior social position must "downplay his advantage out of sensitivity to the junior, while the brother in the 'inferior' position should respect the difference in status. . . . In so doing, each honors the other and unity is preserved."[15] Fraternal ideals were harmony, concord, and unity, which necessitated patience and the practice of forgiveness. Since one's honor was derived from the honor of one's family, individuals in the family had to cooperate for the family's common good rather than for any individual good.

The most frequent designation for the audience of Hebrews is the family epithet, "brothers" (ἀδελφοί *adelphoi*; Heb. 2:11, 12, 17; 3:1, 12; 10:19; 13:22–23).[16] Although "brothers" and other terms of fictive kinship were common designations in ancient Mediterranean society,[17] the Christian usage of the term is distinct because of its theological provenance. The designation "brother" stems from the audience's relationship with God the Father and God the Son, Jesus. The citation of Psalm 8:5–7 in Hebrews 2:5–8 connects the destiny of God's Son with the destiny of humanity because the Son of God took on blood and flesh (2:14, 17) in order to be perfected—made competent for his priestly service—through suffering (2:10). In this way, Jesus could fulfill the Melchizedekian high priestly ministry of being a merciful and faithful high priest who destroys the one who holds the power of death (2:14–15), makes atonement for the sins of the people (2:17), helps those who are tempted (2:18), and leads his younger siblings to glory (2:10). By virtue of their faith in Jesus, believers become "holy brothers" (2:17; 9:26; 10:14, 29).

In sum, the term "brothers" in Hebrews surpasses the metaphoric relationship of close associates or mere biological connection. Rather, "ἀδελφοί is . . . used as a self-designation for those for whom Jesus died, in order to stress once more the commonalities between Jesus and his ἀδελφοί."[18] As the paradigmatic elder brother, Jesus downplayed his own advantage and used it to honor and promote his younger siblings. This designation reminds the audience that their suffering, which is causing them to wane in their commitment, has been experienced to a much greater degree by Jesus, who was victorious. For this reason, he is merciful and is able to help those who are tempted (2:17–18). The familial designation also reminds them of their responsibilities to help and honor one another and to act rightly toward Jesus so that they do not dishonor him (6:6; 10:29). This expansion on the special relatedness of the family of God and its implications for believers is unique to the New Testament.[19]

The migrant camp of the people of God. Just as the individual's worth was defined by the family, so also the family's worth was connected to ethnic ties and country or land. These elements form the matrix that determines the given honor and social standing of the family, and consequently its members. One's genealogy and lineage determined class, status, and trade opportunities. Another motif that pervades the communal identity in Hebrews is as the "migrant camp of the people of God."[20] This self-understanding highlighted the common status of the community as (1) sharing the same ethnic identity and (2) sharing the same social status of foreigner. Roman citizenship brought several entitlements and distinctions that affected all areas of life, such as business (holding property, establishing contracts, and paying taxes), domestic affairs (marriage, having children as natural-born citizens, and making wills), and litigation (courts, custody, and punishments). "[T]he citizen was accorded better treatment than was the imperial subject who did not possess the franchise."[21] In parallel, the Christian foreigner was at risk of losing privileges and rights he might have otherwise enjoyed on account of his faith (e.g., 10:32–34). This group perception brought a sense of responsibility for each member in order to compensate for society's hostility.

The consistent use of metaphors of movement and migration in the exhortation passages elucidates that Christianity is a communal journey. As such, it requires communal solidarity. They journey toward salvation (2:1–4), rest (3:1–4:13), perfection (5:11–6:20), the promise (11:39), Mount Zion (12:25–27), and the heavenly city (13:14). The danger is disorientation by neglect and drift (2:1–4), unbelief and disobedience (3:1–4:13), falling away (6:6), yielding to discouragement (sin, 12:4), and the comfort of the earthly city (13:14). They must therefore imitate or avoid the examples of the past—those who broke the law (2:2), the wilderness generation (3:1–19), Abraham and his generation (6:12–15), their leaders (13:7), the heroes of the faith, and Esau (11:1–40; 12:16–17).[22] During this journey, these migrants can approach the throne of grace through Christ in the heavenly sanctuary to receive the timely help, the grace, and the mercy needed to reach their destination (4:16; 6:19; 7:25).

The significance of group designations for communal solidarity. The significance of conceiving the group's identity as both the family and migrant people of God is that it anchors responsibility for the care of one another in the two universal legitimations of family and ethnic identity. Viewing fellow Christians as one's siblings engenders both greater expectations of and a greater sense of duty toward them. Since family members must be loyal, devoted, and cooperative for the family's honor, this recuperation of the motif in the church prescribes the highest model of communal solidarity. Likewise, the motif of the migrant people of God gives an ethos of communal solidarity of close bonds of kinship similar to that of family. "Brothers" is not used as a mere common term of address, but it is the ultimate legitimation to model how this community must care for one another according to the pattern of care of the "ancestors of the family" (1:1; 2:16; 11:1–12:1). The standard of family duty is set by Jesus, who spared nothing for his siblings. Likewise, brothers and sisters will imitate Jesus's pattern in their "embodied" devotion (ἐν σώματι, *en sōmati*, in the body, 13:3) to the needs of the rest of the family.

The Ethical Ramifications of Spiritual Familial Relationships: Spiritual Oversight and Encouragement

Having considered the terms of address in the Christian family, we saw that the precarious state of the community of Hebrews was counterbalanced by its identity as the family of God. We now turn to the specific behaviors related to this identity that were encouraged by the pastor in order to foster perseverance. Their successful cohesion as a persecuted cognitive minority was aided by their ethical commitments and necessitated pastoral oversight and encouragement. These will be discussed first, followed by how their legitimation of family solidarity created a new cultic worship.

A persecuted cognitive minority: the significance of otherwise unimpressive ethical demands. In his article about the ethics of Hebrews, James W. Thompson makes this opening statement:

> Although the author of Hebrews describes his work as a "word
> of exhortation" (13:22), he offers remarkably few specific
> guidelines for the behavior of his readers. Until chapter 13, the
> author's primary hortatory focus is that the readers "hold on"
> (κατέχειν, 3:6, 14; 10:23; κρατεῖν, 4:14; 6:18) and "draw near"
> (προσέρχεσθαι, 4:16; 7:25; 10:1, 22; 12:18, 22) rather than fall
> away (2:3; 3:12; 6:4–6; 10:26–31).[23]

While most of the ethical imperatives of Hebrews are found in its final chapter, it offers far more than a few rules for its audience. Much of the exhortation (13:22) of the letter comes from the pastor's reassurance that the new covenant, ratified by Jesus, is superior to the old covenant. It also stems from the implications of this assertion on the lives of Jesus's younger siblings in reinforcing their Christian identity. Thompson's pronouncement does not recognize the pastor's admonishment that his hearers exercise spiritual oversight over one another (3:12–13; 4:1; 6:9–12; 10:24–25; 12:1, 12–17). This sense of responsibility is particularly significant because the Christians addressed by Hebrews were what Berger calls a "cognitive minority."[24] It seems that one of the greatest needs that the hearers of Hebrews had was to band together in order to reinforce the plausibility of their "deviant knowledge." They had to be a family that persisted together. The need to cluster together is thus legitimated in the self-perception of the group as a family (they meet together) and as a migrant people (they journey together).

The necessity of spiritual oversight and encouragement. The necessity to exercise spiritual oversight and to encourage one another is observable, though indirectly, in the warning passages of the book of Hebrews. The fear induced by the warning charges them to oversee that their migrating siblings remain within safe boundaries. In addition, direct remarks that exhort the family of God to exercise spiritual oversight and to encourage one another are peppered throughout the text of Hebrews (3:12–13; 4:1; 6:9–12; 10:24–25; 12:1, 12–17, 12:28–13:21). In 3:12, the pastor commands his hearers, since they are a family (ἀδελφοί, *adelphoi*, brothers), to exercise spiritual oversight over one another so that no attitude of unbelief or hard-heartedness takes root among them (3:12–13). The command is not merely to "watch out" (βλέπετε, *blepete*) in a defensive manner, but to constructively "encourage one another day by day." The goal is that "none of you become hardened by the deception of sin" (3:13 LEB). In 3:16–19, the pastor reminds his audience that the core problem of those who died in the desert was unbelief (alluding to Num. 14). He infers from this period in Israel's history (οὖν, *oun*, therefore, 4:1) that the lesson to be learned for the present people of God is "let us fear if, while a promise remains of entering His rest, any one of you may seem to have come short of it" (4:1 NASB). The group as a whole must exercise oversight over "some of you [second person plural]" (τις ἐξ ὑμῶν, *tis ex hymōn*) who seem to be falling short of the promise.

In Hebrews 5:10–14, the problem of the audience is its sluggishness in "hearing" the "hard message" of the Melchizedekian priesthood of Jesus and, ultimately, its lack of maturity. In 6:9–12, the pastor resumes speaking to the audience in the second person (as opposed to the indirect and severe third person description of "those" who are impossible to renew to repentance in 6:4–8). These verses reassure the audience of its salvation (6:9). The reason (γάρ, *gar*, for) the preacher gives for his confidence in this matter is the love the audience has shown for God's name in their past and present service to the saints (6:10). The pastor suggests from this development marker (δέ, *de*, and/but), marking a progression, that part of the cure for the hearers' sluggishness is the resurgence of their former zeal. He commands them to "show the same diligence" as before (6:11 NASB). The result of this communal devotion to one another is that it will foster "the fulfillment of your hope until the end" (6:11 NET), and the community of Hebrews will be "imitators of those who through faith and perseverance inherit the promises" (6:12 NET). Their spiritual problem (5:11–14) is, in part, solved by a renewed display of community solidarity to the saints through practical help (10:32–35; 13:1–6). "Sticking it out" as spiritual siblings will go a long way and will even revive their devotion to Jesus.

In 10:19–25, the pastor draws inferences from his extended argument that concerns the high priesthood of Christ. The third hortatory subjunctive is a call to "take thought of how to spur one another on to love and good works" (10:24 NET). The author defines how they can do so through two contrasted present participles (10:25). The first, by "not abandoning our own forsaking together" (NASB), defines what will impede the migrating family's love and good works. The banding together of Christians is necessary to maintain strong social stability. In contrast (ἀλλά, *alla*, but rather), they must continually encourage one another. Christian gatherings reinforce Christian identity, while Christian estrangement weakens one's Christian identity.

In 12:11–17, the author draws (διό, *dio*, for this reason) practical implications from looking at persecution as God's fatherly discipline to children (12:1–10), remarking that "all discipline seems painful at the time, not joyful" (12:11 NET). The pain of persecution was tempting some to leave the race (12:12) and had nearly caused some (vv. 15–16, τις, *tis*) to abandon the race (vv. 12–14). Some within the community were agents of disruption (v. 16), while others had become immoral and worldly (v. 17). These rebellious "sons" are compared with the archetypal "bad son," Esau, who did not choose suffering "for the joy set before him" but rather sold his birthright "for one meal" (12:16). Esau, although he wanted to "inherit the blessing" and sought it with tears, was rejected because he did not repent (5:7–8; 12:17). Esau's disregard of his inheritance and his choice of transient pleasures over his blessing made it impossible for him to receive it again.[25] The pastor communicates that his audience faces a similar danger and charges them with spiritual oversight to address negative behavior and with the ministry of encouragement.

In summary, the sociology of knowledge helps us see that, as a cognitive minority, it was necessary for this community to continually reinforce itself concerning the truth of its faith and to root out what was not conducive to perseverance. This survey of Hebrews 3:12–13; 4:1; 6:9–12; 10:24–25; 12:1, 12–17 shows that the work is peppered with imperatives for its audience (1) to exercise spiritual oversight and uproot sinful attitudes from among them and (2) to reinforce one another through encouragement. The assumption of the pastor seems to be that without the siblings' mutual spiritual oversight and encouragement, unbelieving tendencies would spring up, some would fall away from the living God, and others would display destructive community behavior such as sexual misconduct (12:16; 13:4).

An example of the specific mechanisms of what is reinforced through this banding together would be how the theology of Hebrews provides an alternative to the dominant culture's definition of shame and honor, as David A. deSilva argues. The imitation of the examples listed in 10:32–12:3 (the audience's former days, 10:32–39; the faithful ancients, 11:1–40; Jesus, 12:1–3) will lead to honor in the eyes of God, the one to whom everyone must give an account (4:13). DeSilva explains that "it is in association with one's fellow Christians that one reinforces and is reinforced in the distinctive values of that culture, commends and receives commendation for acting out these values and advancing toward peculiarly Christian goals."[26] The local church (10:25) provides the plausibility structure where Christians find value and approval for their deviant knowledge. In doing so, it contradicts society's shaming of Christians. Yet this reinforcing mechanism is only operative insofar as Christians huddle together, exercise spiritual oversight, and encourage one another.

The admonitions of Hebrews regarding spiritual oversight and encouragement may not be extraordinary ethical cases, but insofar as the objective of the pastor was to encourage this congregation to persevere, these exhortations were on target. The fellowship of the family of God acts as a countercultural community that "provides continuing therapy against the creeping doubt as to whether, after all, one may not be wrong and the majority right."[27]

The new cultic worship: a legitimation of family solidarity. Hebrews 12:28 offers a summary of the exhortation in 12:25–27, beginning with the phrase, "therefore, [since we are] receiving an unshakable kingdom."[28] This phrase frames the context of a new topic—namely the ethical implications of this kingdom to be inherited.[29] The two hortatory subjunctives, "let us give thanks, and through this let us offer worship pleasing to God"

(v. 28 NET), are the theme of the conclusion of Hebrews (12:28–13:21): pleasing (εὐαρέστως, *heyarestōs*) [cultic] service. This "hook word" (εὐαρέστως) in 12:28 and its cognates in 13:16, 21 hold the section together. Through the imperatives of 13:1–19, "pleasing cultic service" is redefined and contextualized for Christians "in these last days" (1:2). The section is then concluded by a benediction of the speaker—it is God who will equip them to do what is pleasing (13:21, τὸ εὐάρεστον, *to heuareston*).[30]

The shift in focus from cultic worship in 12:28–29; 13:10–16 to concrete life in 13:1–6, 16 draws attention to the paradoxical relationship between the two themes. The inference between the juxtaposition of these two dissimilar subjects is that "there must not be separation anymore, but identification."[31] The priestly service of the Christian community does not consist of activities in the tabernacle, but of practical help among brothers and sisters. What appear to be mundane exhortations in 13:1–6 do, in fact, refer to the sacrifices that are pleasing to God (12:28; 13:16). To worship God is to "love the brothers" (13:1). The new sacrifices of the temple are actions that share the needs of the members of the community and good works (13:16). The superiority of the new covenant not only prevents the hearers from going back to their former beliefs, but also reorients their religious practices toward the needs of God's family. The author of Hebrews makes communal solidarity sacred through cultic language. In the new covenant, the temple sacrifices have become what one does for the service of the saints (6:10; 13:16). This love, practically expressed for one another, will help the community endure the abuses of the outside world. This mutual love is crucial because the call of the Christian life leads to rejection by society (13:10–14) and places believers in a position of both cognitive minority and socioeconomic hardship.

If one has built his own identity through the frame of reference of the theology of Hebrews, then the world becomes an "ethical world" in which any act made in service to the family has a sacred cultic significance. Backhaus poignantly states:

> [T]he common world of early Christians—their worshiping,
> their self-awareness as described in the *homologia* [confession],

their solidarity under pressure, and their practical *koinonia* [fellowship] in everyday life—takes part in the great drama between heaven and earth performed by the Son and high priest Jesus Christ.[32]

This is the contribution of Hebrews to New Testament ethics: because of its magnificent theology (Heb. 1–12), a simple deed such as offering a ride back from "our own meetings" (10:25 NET) to a youngster whose parents mock his nascent faith has the utmost cultic significance—one greater than the tabernacle's sacrifices ever had.

Summary

This chapter has looked at how the theology of Hebrews defines the community as the family of God and as God's migrant people. This communal identity establishes the duties of each member in relation to his or her brothers and sisters. The limits of this service are set by the elder brother, Jesus, who offered himself up for the rest of the family. The pastor, who knew the precarious condition of some within the community, directs certain ethical demands toward behaviors that uphold the plausibility structure of the church. The community had to band together closely, exercise spiritual oversight, and encourage one another in order to resist the assimilation attempts of the cognitive majority. When the assembly is together, it "enables individuals to internalize specifically Christian standards of practice."[33] On a practical level, the pastor provides a powerful legitimation for communal solidarity by equating practical support with a superior cultic significance than the acts of worship in the tabernacle of the Old Covenant. This compensates for the social and economic losses that come from being a Christian. Thus, for the author of Hebrews, one's identity as a member of the family of God was the *sine qua non* to foster perseverance in faith and communal solidarity.

What might an identity as a member of the family of God, then, do to one's "churchgoing" habits? Let us return to my friend, who thought that a Christian could do without "going to church." Is there anything valuable in her criticism with which the author of Hebrews would agree? If a given church offers no relational depth and communal solidarity that is similar to that of a healthy blood family, then "going to church" is not as profitable as it could be. On the other hand, to what aspects of my friend's argument would the preacher object? He would not accept the possibility that one could live as a child of God apart from the other children of God. He would argue that Christian identity necessitates fellowship with the family of God, as well as the spiritual oversight, encouragement, and communal solidarity that it entails. A member of the family of God possesses an identity that is necessarily communal: you do not choose your siblings; you cling to them, persevering with them, according to the love pattern of your elder brother, Jesus.

According to the author of Hebrews, since Christians joined the family of God, there must be relational depth and communal solidarity among them. This self-identification is necessary to anchor the ethics of nurturing relationships, oversight, encouragement, and accountability. Christian gatherings are family gatherings—"behold, I and the children God has given me" (2:13 LEB). Christians must carry out the extent of their devotion to their siblings in Christ, just as they would for their blood family in the Greco-Roman world of the New Testament. This raises the following question for all churches throughout the ages: Do our formal gatherings allow the theological reality (e.g., Christians are siblings in Christ) to become effectual (e.g., developing a level of commitment and intimacy that makes this real)? With this vision of personal and communal identity, one does not just leave the local church, but rather abandons his brothers and sisters. While it is possible to leave a physical place ("I don't go to church there anymore"), one cannot leave a family; one can only abandon his or her family. Hebrews challenges "church members" to see themselves as a family. Hebrews exhorts those who lead the assembly (13:7, 17) to do so in a way in which the healthy family dynamics of spiritual oversight, nurturing relationships, encouragement, and solidarity can be expressed. This outlook challenges Christians to think of the issue of "leaving my local church" with the same seriousness with which one would consider severing their relationship with their parents or divorcing. This, of course, presumes that one develops family-like relationships with his church brothers and sisters. This mind-set transforms the church from a place that dispenses a service to a place where an individual both gives and receives. For both the recipients of Hebrews and for us, church participation is about ensuring that all the brothers and sisters continue on the journey and persevere to the end, with a sound faith (which presumes spiritual oversight and encouragement) and with their physical needs met. If one leaves a congregation without a sense of loss by both the departed and the church, this testifies to a failure of the individual to invest and develop nurturing relationships with his or her siblings in Christ and of the congregation's failure to provide a nurturing and healthy family environment. In sum, we see that without a personal identity as a member of the family of God, we allow "church" to be an activity that can be done and not the complete family experience that it is intended to be. This should lead us to think carefully about the vocabulary we use to describe our church practices ("going to church," "she's a dear sister," "doing church," "programs," etc.) and to consider if the reality behind these terms is being honored.

If the author of Hebrews could question me, perhaps he would ask, "How are the family dynamics in your local assembly? Are they healthy? Is there spiritual oversight, encouragement, and practical solidarity—all done in love? Is there space for the brothers and sisters to share, confess, and encourage each other?" If the preacher could question my friend, perhaps he would ask, "Are you an orphan of God or a child of God? Are you really sure that as a child of God, you have nothing to contribute to your siblings in Christ? They need you. You need them to grow and fully live out your identity in Christ."

NOTES

[1] Hebrews defines itself as a "word of exhortation" (12:5; 13:22), an expression featured in Acts 13:15, 1 Timothy 4:13, and 2 Maccabees 15:8–11. Further, the author commands the recipients to exhort one another (3:13), which presupposes a congregational setting (10:24), hence "confirming the homiletic character of Hebrews." One also notes the abundant verbs of "speaking": the addressees are not readers but hearers, and the author is primarily portrayed as speaking to them (2:5; 5:11; 6:9; 8:1; 9:5; 11:32). David E. Aune, *The New Testament in Its Literary Environment* (Philadelphia: Westminster, 1985), 212–13.

[2] Peter L. Berger, *The Sacred Canopy* (New York: Doubleday, 1967); Peter L. Berger and Thomas Luckmann, *The Social Construction of Reality: A Treatise in the Sociology of Knowledge* (New York: Doubleday, 1966).

[3] Berger and Luckmann, *Social Construction of Reality*, 1.

[4] David G. Horrell, *Solidarity and Difference: Reading of Paul's Ethics*, 2nd ed. (New York: Bloomsbury, 2016), 92.

[5] Berger, *Sacred Canopy*, 29.

[6] Berger, 33.

[7] Berger and Luckmann, *Social Construction of Reality*, 120.

[8] Berger, *Sacred Canopy*, 45.

[9] Berger, 48.

[10] Berger, 8.

[11] Bryan R. Dyer, "Suffering in the Face of Death: The Social Context of the Epistle to the Hebrews" (PhD diss., McMaster Divinity College, 2015), iv.

[12] Craig R. Koester, *Hebrews: Translation with Introduction and Commentary* (New York: Doubleday, 2001), 64–72.

[13] Mark McVann, "Family-Centeredness," in *Handbook of Biblical Social Values*, ed. John J. Pilch and Bruce J. Malina (Eugene, OR: Cascade, 2016), 64.

[14] David A. deSilva, *Honor, Patronage, Kinship and Purity: Unlocking New Testament Culture* (Downers Grove, IL: InterVarsity Press, 2010), 166.

[15] DeSilva, *Honor, Patronage, Kinship and Purity*, 168. DeSilva comments on *De fraterno amore* 487A–B.

[16] Ἀγαπητοί is used once and connotes a similar meaning (6:9). The indication is that it "pertains to one who is dearly loved . . . indicating a close relationship, especially that between parent and child." See Walter Bauer, *A Greek-English Lexicon of the New Testament and Other Early Christian Literature (BDAG)*, ed. Frederick W. Danker (Chicago: University of Chicago Press, 2000), 7. The audience is also designated as believers (4:3), as saints (6:10; 13:24), and as refugees (6:18). Paul Trebilco, *Self-Designations and Group Identity in the New Testament* (New York: Cambridge University Press, 2012), 113, 50. The occurrences of ἀδελφός in 7:5 and 8:11 are not included, since they are not used as terms of address in these two verses.

[17] Craig S. Keener, "Family and Household," in *Dictionary of New Testament Background: A Compendium of Contemporary Biblical Scholarship*, ed. Craig A. Evans and Stanley E. Porter (Downers Grove, IL: InterVarsity, 2000), 354.

[18] Trebilco, *Self-Designations*, 55.

[19] Trebilco, 56.

[20] The "wandering people of God" as a motif was put forward first by Ernst K. Käsemann, *Das Wandernde Gottesvolk: Eine Untersuchung Zum Hebräerbrief* (Göttingen: Vandenhoeck & Ruprecht, 1939). This theme has been refined in Annang Asumang and Bill Domeris, "The Migrant Camp of the People of God: Theme for the Epistle to the Hebrews," *Conspectus* 3, no. 1 (2007): 6.

[21] Brian M. Rapske, "Citizenship, Roman," in *Dictionary of New Testament Background: A Compendium of Contemporary Biblical Scholarship*, ed. Craig A. Evans and Stanley E. Porter (Downers Grove, IL: InterVarsity, 2000), 215.

[22] Asumang and Domeris, "Migrant Camp," 11–13.

[23] James W. Thompson, "Insider Ethics for Outsiders: Ethics for Aliens in Hebrews," *Restoration Quarterly* 53, no. 4 (2011): 207.

[24] Peter L. Berger, *A Rumor of Angels: Modern Society and the Rediscovery of the Supernatural* (New York: Doubleday, 1969), 7.

[25] George H. Guthrie, "Hebrews," in *Commentary on the New Testament Use of the Old Testament*, ed. G. K. Beale and D. A. Carson (Grand Rapids, MI: Baker Academic, 2007), 985.

[26] David A. deSilva, *Despising Shame: Honor Discourse and Community Maintenance in the Epistle to the Hebrews*, rev. ed. (Atlanta: Society of Biblical Literature, 2008), 308–9.

[27] Berger, *Rumor of Angels*, 22.

[28] Author's translation.

[29] Steven E. Runge, *Discourse Grammar of the Greek New Testament: A Practical Introduction for Teaching and Exegesis* (Peabody, MA: Hendrickson, 2011), 210.

[30] Joshua Caleb Hutchens, "Christian Worship in Hebrews 12:28 as Ethical and Exclusive," *Journal of the Evangelical Theological Society* 59, no. 3 (2016): 522; Craig R. Koester, "Hebrews, Rhetoric, and the Future," in *Reading the Epistle to the Hebrews: A Resource for Students*, ed. Eric F. Mason and Kevin B. McCruden (Atlanta: Society of Biblical Literature, 2011), 117; Père Albert Vanhoye, "La Question Littéraire De Hébreux Xiii. 1–6," *New Testament Studies* 23, no. 2 (1977): 139.

[31] Author's translation. "La Question Littéraire," 139.

[32] Knut Backhaus, "How to Entertain Angels: Ethics in the Epistle to the Hebrews," in *Hebrews: Contemporary Methods-New Insights*, ed. Gabriella Gelardini (Boston: Brill, 2005), 168.

[33] Backhaus, "How to Entertain Angels," 169.

PART TWO

Christian Identity and Contemporary Issues

A Theology of Identity
Christian Identity as Migrant

JENNY MCGILL

A lmost 250 million migrants, or 3.4 percent of the world's popu-lation, currently live outside their country of birth or citizenship.[1] While this number continues to rise, the majority of the inhabitants of the world do not move outside their country of birth. The identity for the Christian, on the other hand, should be one of movement, of migration. What term best illustrates this idea?

Words such as *pilgrim, sojourner, alien, exiled, tourist,* and *monk,* among others, have been employed.[2] One may think of Thomas Aquinas's use of *homo viator* (human traveling on the way), John Bunyan's *Pilgrim Progress,* Stanley Hauerwas and William Willimon's *Resident Aliens,* or Rod Dreher's *The Benedict Option,* in which the authors describe the Christian's relative relation to the society in which she is located.[3]

Katherine Harrison Brennan also offers an excellent rationale for why exile is an unhelpful categorization for Christians in the twenty-first century Western world.[4] In this chapter, I explore the term *migrant*, not only to describe the Christian's place in society, but to illustrate one's identity in Christ.

Migrants encounter a multitude of transitions but generally hold a destination in mind. Their path can be circular, unpredictable, or uncharted, but migrants possess a directionality of course. Such is the case with Christian identity. As Christians, our identity is an internal migration, spiritually. One's identity—who one thinks one is—is transformed by one's identification with Christ in his death, burial, and resurrection (Rom. 6). To clarify, I consider the term *migrant* metaphorically, to describe the spiritual transformation of our personal identity as we identify with Christ, and literally, that we are people on the move in the world for Christ. In the following pages, I examine Christian identity as migrational in terms of the nature of its departure, belonging, and displacement.

Understanding one's Christian identity as migrant connotes a journey. A physical sojourn is a purposeful movement toward an attainable goal or achievement.[5] Christians likewise involve a purposeful migration of their identity: a journey to God. The Christian self seeks to love God through obedience to God's commands (John 14:15–31; 1 John 2:4–5), migrates, and is re-created by God's grace through the Holy Spirit. Hauerwas reminds us that Christ's command to follow him called his disciples to step into a journey and to *move* from their present location, not in some self-guided direction but after him.[6] Each follower of Christ, then, decides to become a migrant and to leave one's former sense of self (Matt. 26:40–1; Rom. 7:7–24). This alters the process of self-decision; decisions are made not by the individual alone, but in keeping with Christ's commands and in communion with other believers. This stance radically departs from the philosophies of humanism, secularism, positivism, atheism, and rationalism—all of which share a penchant for self-devotion.[7] The journey is demanding, but for Aquinas, hope helps the traveler to persevere.[8] The Christian identity involves departure, belonging, and displacement. I expound on each of these in turn.

Identity of Departure

The identity of the Christian self involves a departure—the primary departure of allegiance. This departure can take a variety of forms, but it is directed from a point (who one once was) to another destination (who one is in Christ). Those who believe the Christian gospel are swept up into its message and depart from their past beliefs.[9] Their allegiances change. The self, as a determining agent, allows another authority to reign as superordinate, placing itself as God's servant. The outlook of departure is to consider one's life no longer one's own.[10] Obeying Jesus Christ means following him and submitting to his leadership and direction.

Migration within the self occurs by the daily practice of Christian virtues, conforming one's identity into the person of Jesus Christ.[11] In this process of transformation, one learns to flee from worldliness to pursue God,[12] and one's self-understanding is disrupted. For example, when Job questions God, through his socially constructed identities, his true self emerges, as Susannah Ticciati posits.[13] One's self-understanding changes in the disruption; Job, in fact, is the "process of [his] probing."[14] The integrity of one's self, structured by God in election, deepens through this disrupting embodiment.

Since the first migration from the garden of peace, God's people of faith have long demonstrated a pattern of pilgrimage.[15] Abraham's story perhaps best demonstrates this identity of departure based on divine directive; it serves as an example to all who would follow in his faith footsteps (Gen. 12, 15; Rom. 4:11, 16; Heb. 11:2, 8–17). Not only was Abram called to leave his family's religion in a departure of spiritual allegiance; he was also called by God to leave his family's country in a departure of circumstance (Gen.12:1–3).[16] God gave him a clear delineation for obedience: leave to bless and be blessed in return. Abraham, with no known assurance other than belief in a God whose word was reality, moved (Gen. 24:7). Abraham's belief in this revealed God changed his spiritual allegiance, and in his case, this belief not only required a spiritual migration but also a physical migration. All who adopt the Christian faith are also called to an internal spiritual move and to begin a pilgrimage (Ps. 84:5–7).[17] The journey itself is an indication and acknowledgement that the individual needs to be spiritually transformed.

As I have described in my previous work,[18] after conversion an individual undergoes a transformation of self (Gal. 2:19–20). This change does not signify a loss of the original self or of individual distinction, but a change—a movement—in relationality.[19] God was inclined to redeem humanity, and this inclination made relation possible. The human self, for those who accept this relationship, is changed by that determination for relationality, which in turn shapes their identities. Jeremy Gabrielson adeptly describes Saul of Tarsus's transformation as an "enlivening" of, rather than an eradication of, his self. Saul, who became Paul upon his Damascus conversion, was so completely deconstructed and reconstructed in his identification with Christ that he experienced an entire reorientation to his identity, way of life, and mission (Gal. 6:14–15).[20] This kind of dynamic relationship is only made possible by the action of both parties, divine and human. The indwelling of Christ requires human movement—both invitation and participation.

This redefinition of the self in Christ culminates in an adopted identity. The core of the self redetermines and realigns to identify with Christ and his mission. A follower of Christ acknowledges one's old self-maneuvering as an invalid attempt to preserve one's independence from God. In a movement of exchange, one receives a new, redeemed self that the Son of God constrains into a new pattern of life: self-giving. This movement signifies an exchange of identity, of leadership, and of allegiance, but not an exchange of the individual person. The person as a being remains intact and re-created. "Putting on a new self" means that a change—a shift from dressing in the same way as before—is necessary (Eph. 4:24). While individuals possess multiple identities of varying importance, they typically give precedence to one central identity and organize the others in relation to it. They pass all their decisions through the grid of one of these life themes—beauty, faith, family, ethnicity, sexuality, fear—which creates (inconsistencies notwithstanding) a semblance of internal coherence. For the Christian, Christ becomes this definitive agent that determines personal identity.

Upon spiritual conversion or *metanoia*, individuals experience a shift in identity, a change of being, and a turning from who they once were as they attempt to live as liberated creatures of God. This new acknowledgment of dependence indicates a migration. Conversion is a spiritual process in which God calls one to depart and to follow Christ, and this process reorients one's personal identity. Determinant factors of identity, such as relationships (including those with history, society, and family), habits, language, and motivations become subject to Christ. Jesus is the new "environment" in which the Christian moves and, in this geographical sense, in which identity is restructured.[21] In this reconciliation of identity, a synchronous self-configuration occurs, and competing roles and behavior are brought in obedience to Christ. Diachronically, one's identity reconciles different historical experiences of the same self into categories of "before Christ" and "after Christ."[22]

When one identifies with Christ, one joins a collective identity that is composed of every nation, tribe, and tongue and has been grafted into one group called by God to depart from polytheism (Rom. 11:13–24). What is more, they claim allegiance to their manner of belief and living as revealed by Israel's history and Messiah.[23] As it is their formal acknowledgment that they have been claimed, the emphasis of their departure is not so much in the perfection of their faithfulness (although that is an expected due course) but rather in the truthfulness of their lives. They claim their identity as followers in a resolute posture of dependence and trust.

Whereas this departure of allegiance is intrinsic to the Christian identity, one's physical departure varies by circumstance. A variety of factors drive individuals to migrate—God's particular calling, environmental disasters, family connections, and personal desires. Cultural expectations, family pressures, and competing desires can also influence the direction of the departure one takes. Given the human condition to err, even though one may seek to follow God's will on one's journey, the path of obedience for each individual is by no means linear and is often circuitous. Their progress unfolds over time and often in hindsight.[24] Moltmann reinforces the teleological element of this departure in his characterization of nature. For the person set on pilgrimage, nature becomes one's "traveling companion." Both nature and the pilgrim yearn in faith, with hope for the culmination of God's kingdom rather than the transitory present (Rom. 8:18–22; 2 Cor. 4). Moltmann writes that both humans and creation view "the world . . . as a process moving in a unified fashion toward its redemption."[25] Beyond Moltmann's analogy, more significantly, the Spirit of God remains the Christian's traveling companion throughout the course of life (John 14:16, 26; 15:26; John 16:7; Eph. 1:13). The fact that God accompanies and directs the transformation of the self on this journey assures its completion (Phil. 1:6). This change is a complex, dynamic process that follows a unique path for each person in one's daily and ultimate conversion from behavioral and psychological darkness to light (John 8:12; Acts 26:18; 2 Cor. 4:6; Eph. 5:8; 1 Pet. 2:9; 1 John 2:9).

Identity of Belonging

This departure indicates the commencement of a journey, but the pilgrimage of personhood is more than a departure and a beginning; it is a belonging. In order to create this belonging, the identity of departure requires that every part of one's being becomes identified with and found in Christ. The self's transformational journey culminates in a reunion with God. Ultimately, as Alpha and Omega, God is both the beginning of and the end of self-pilgrimage.

The first migration of identity for the self is one of belonging; the Christian undergoes a transfer of identity by adoption, in which one is received into a new family. The self's new location becomes in Christ and placed into his lineage; the Christian self lives outside itself and in God upon conversion.[26] This element of belonging—that the self is held in God—is crucial. Other stimuli continue to shape the person, but the self is defined by God. Experiences are subjected to this greater reality: who I am is defined by whose I am. Since God assigns meaning, one's personal identity "arises *extra se*," outside of oneself.[27]

The second migration that creates this identity of belonging concerns God's divine presence. God's Spirit condescends to indwell persons (1 Cor. 3:16). Although the exchange is unevenly weighted, it still demonstrates reciprocity and mutual belonging between humanity and God. As the sacrament of baptism portrays, the Christian pilgrimage involves a daily journey of reconciliation with the triune God. The goal of this new life is to commune with God, and this communion directs the pilgrim. The intimacy of that communion allows the pilgrim to walk in obedience to God

(Matt. 5:48; 1 Pet. 1:16). The new self portrays God's likeness, and the character of the triune God determines the Christian's identity.[28]

The identity of belonging indicates a familial relationship. This relationship shows a positional belonging when Christians are reborn, adopted as heirs of God's kingdom, experientially belong to Christ, and join one particular narrative. Anyone born outside of a family has no permanent place in that family, but a son or daughter belongs to it forever. This permanent sense of belonging is a result of this family relationship. While parents can disinherit their children socially and legally, and children can emancipate themselves from their parents' authority, family members cannot become unrelated to each other. In an even deeper commitment, God has vowed to never disinherit those who accept their adopted identity (2 Tim. 2:13). Herein is the dynamic exchange between parties—the steadfastness of God's loyal giving and the self's unpredictable receiving. Even if God divinely knows which children will stray, God does not wish to control their actions. In addition to belonging to God the Father as children and belonging in God the Christ, the Christian identity of belonging also includes the last member of the Trinity: God the Spirit (Rom. 8:15; Gal. 4:6). Through belief in "the word of truth" in Christ, the Christian self is given God's Spirit, which is "a deposit guaranteeing [its] inheritance until the redemption of those who are God's possession" (Eph. 1:13–14). God's accompanying Spirit serves as one's "chaperone" on life's journey, until the final reunion and the ultimate fulfillment of the self.[29]

This identity of belonging relates to the eschatological promise of God's kingdom. Who one will be in the future informs one's present identity, and what will be in the future motivates one's present behavior. This teleological understanding of promised history undergirds an understanding of Christian identity.[30] God's promise to redeem creation and consummate its deliverance guides one's understanding of how to exist. When Christians believe that they belong to this promise, they understand who they are, where they come from, and how they should act and react.[31] One's identity—who one perceives oneself to be—is the birthplace of willed action and prescribes how that individual will interact with the other.[32] How does one accept the other yet differentiate the self from the other? How does one seek self-protection and also reconciliation? How does one fight injustice yet remember wrongs suffered rightly? How do warring communities pursue peace? God's eschatological promise and a Christian identity of belonging offer answers to these questions.

One's Christian identity comes from belonging to God, but it is also colored by one's culture. Who the self is and what identity it portrays primarily reflects its God-given nature within a finite historical milieu. Even though they are scarred by the fall, cultures display God's creative imagination when it is placed in humanity's hands. Despite the presence of sin, cultures display wonderful ingenuity in their mores, infrastructure, communication patterns, art, and so on. The Christian self belongs to God fully and to its culture illustratively. As Campbell rightly shares, "Christ-identity can pervade all cultures, transforming them but not imperialistically obliterating everything as if Christian faith were an entirely independent culture which replaces, and is discontinuous with, previously existing patterns of life."[33] Cultural ideals do not trump the Christian's responsibility to belong to God (in manner of pattern, speech, and thought) when and where these conflict. Although people are born into cultural settings that deeply impact their patterns of thinking, speech, and behavior, their regenerated being creates a new identity that is formed by God's Spirit, Word, and church. This communal shaping evidences the self's identity of belonging.

The Christian self acknowledges a dependence on a divine God and understands the purpose of a socially constructed self. The Christian self develops precisely through a process of socialization that includes the innervation of God's Spirit and the influence of groups such as one's family and church. Rather than reveling in unattachment, Christians are called to be deeply tied to each other, to be bound by faith even more than by nation. This sense of belonging can profoundly affect the migration experience of the Christian, for as a member of one global church, the migrant has relatives around the world.[34] Additionally, Hauerwas cautions that this collection may easily become enchanted with political affiliations and earthly kingdoms, losing its sense of separateness and participation in God's kingdom (1 Pet. 1:1). As Christians, a group of strangers are being transformed into one identity and one communion as the body of Christ, and together they migrate expectantly toward the Eschaton.[35] The

Christian, then, is a migrant in one's self-formation and as a member of the church community.

Identity of Displacement

The redeemed self belongs to God in a new manner of living. The self after conversion possesses two qualities in greater fullness: an increased capacity to give of oneself and a new openness in oneself that allows the other a presence. These qualities lead to a rich, vibrant, ever-changing, and unpredictable construal of identity. This arrangement maintains the essential distinction of the individual, avoids the dissolution of the self, and allows the other to be identified in the self as part of its identity as a "non-identity."[36] Furthermore, the rapprochement of the self and the other disarms the power struggle within the self, which is practical in today's culture of power politics, economic scarcities, gender wars, and ethnic rivalries. The self recoils from injuring itself; when the self perceives the other as part of itself, it pauses. When the other is integral to one's identity and self, the other is no longer the enemy.

Because it belongs to God, the self gains the capacity to consider the other in a new way. If the other is no longer an enemy, the self feels a responsibility to protect the other as a fellow creature of God. If Christian identity must reflect Jesus Christ, then a Christian will not only identify with his death, burial, and resurrection but with his displacement of self (Phil. 2:3–6). Not only will the redeemed self acknowledge and receive the other, but it will displace itself for the other and choose to be alienated for the other. Paul imitated Christ when he experienced and taught a consistent self-shifting for the sake of the other (Rom. 12:10; 1 Cor. 9:21–23).

The story of Joseph demonstrates these three facets of a Christian identity. Joseph's kidnapping thrust him into a foreign world of Egyptian customs and gods at an impressionable age. From approximately age seventeen through age thirty, he lived as a member of an ethnic and religious minority, suffering both antagonism and socioeconomic oppression (Gen. 37:2; 41:46; 43:32). He learned, however, how to operate within this environment, speaking their dialect and assuming their forms of appearance, to the extent that his own brothers did not recognize him (Gen. 42:8, 23). While these years of Egyptian socialization could have influenced him to forget his people's faith in Yahweh, Joseph demonstrated an identity of departure from his surrounding influences. Joseph did not forsake his allegiance to, and identification with, this foreign God of the Hebrews. Second, Joseph feared and enjoyed a communion with God that demonstrated an identity of belonging—one that was so obvious that others attested to it (Gen. 41:38; 42:18). Joseph derived personal meaning from relating to his God (Gen. 39:9; 45:7–8). Most of all, Joseph's encounter with his brothers demonstrated an identity of displacement. After they betrayed him at such a vulnerable age, Joseph easily could have severed any further contact with his brothers when they were driven to Egypt by famine. Yet he created space within himself, displaced his personal wounds, and extended himself to the very ones who had sold him into slavery. After almost fifteen years apart, he could not have predicted how his brothers would respond to his kind overtures. Even though he risked incredible pain if his brothers were not remorseful, Joseph set aside his prior victimization in the hope of reconciliation.

This willed displacement is a twofold migration of the self. The self makes a circumstantial choice to make room for the other, and in doing so, that very self is moved (shaped) internally.[37] Clemens Sedmak describes this ability to be displaced a chief capacity.[38] The dynamics of being out of place are transformative, leading the individual on a journey in which "epistemic resilience," the drawing upon inner resources to withstand and engage external threat, is paramount.[39] Is alienation in a given culture detrimental to one's sense of identity? For example, did the exiled Jewish population retain their religious identity more faithfully than those who remained in Judah (Jer. 24:4–7)? Jehu Hanciles argues this convincingly.[40] Is Christian identity, then, better refined and preserved from a position of displacement and minority status?

Last Thoughts

As Christians, a local, regional, national, and global church, make sense of who we are in a changing world, let us remember that personal identity is subjected to Christ through others in the body of Christ (Rom. 12:5). We are Christians as individuals, but this label only possesses meaning because of the One to whom we are joined together.

In any given situation, how do we relate our Christian identity as one of departure, belonging, and displacement or a varied composite? This requires a careful consideration of the performance—of both "separating and binding," "embracing and distancing," as Miroslav Volf has articulated so well—through personal study and practice and local church accountability and worship.[41] Whether we hold a cultural position of majority power, or lose said power, or have never experienced it, our movement should be within our self-understanding to move toward those marginalized, even as we are called to also move away from those claiming the name of Christ falsely (1 Cor. 5; 1 John 2:18–27, 4:1–6). We are people on the move toward the place God is preparing for us (John 14:2–4) with eager and desperate hope for the great homecoming. May we choose daily to bend low (1 Pet. 5:6) and be the first to move toward loving God and others in our self-understanding.

NOTES

[1] Global Knowledge Partnership on Migration and Development, *Migration and Remittances: Recent Developments and Outlook* (Washington, DC: The World Bank, April 2016), http://pubdocs.worldbank.org/en/661301460400427908/Migrationand DevelopmentBrief26.pdf.

[2] William T. Cavanaugh, "Migrant, Tourist, Pilgrim, Monk: Mobility and Identity in a Global Age," *Theological Studies* 69, no. 2 (2008): 340–56.

[3] David Elliot, "The Christian as Homo Viator: A Resource in Aquinas for Overcoming 'Worldly Sin and Sorrow,'" *Journal of the Society of Christian Ethics* 34, no. 2 (2014): 101–21.

[4] Katherine Harrison Brennan, "No Place for Exile: How Christians Should (Not) Make Sense of Their Place in the World," *Australian Broadcasting Corporation,* December 16, 2016, http://www.abc.net.au/religion/articles/2016/12/16/4593491.htm.

[5] I refer here to voluntary migration rather than forced migration. Still, even those moved involuntarily remain under God's care.

[6] See the repeated commands given by Jesus to follow him: Matt. 4:19; 8:22; 9:9; 10:38; 16:24; 19:21; Mark 1:17; 2:14; John 1:43; 10:27; 12:26; 21:19, 22. Note his injunction of whom not to follow: Luke 21:8.

[7] Stanley Hauerwas and William Willimon, *Resident Aliens: Life in the Christian Colony* (Nashville: Abingdon, 1989), 49–50.

[8] Elliot, "Christian as Homo Viator," 104, 108.

[9] The message of the Christian gospel is primarily to believe in Jesus Christ. In believing in the Christ, one accepts that s/he has personally transgressed the holiness and goodness of God and, through Christ's physical crucifixion, burial, and resurrection, which satisfied the wrath of God on one's behalf, one's sin has been propitiated, communion has been restored with God, and freedom to walk in newness of life following the way of Jesus has been inaugurated.

[10] Stanley Hauerwas, *Christian Existence Today: Essays on Church, World, and Living in Between* (Durham, NC: Labyrinth, 1988), 91.

[11] Frederick Christian Bauerschmidt, "Thomas Aquinas: The Unity of the Virtues and the Journeying Self," in *Unsettling Arguments: A Festschrift on the Occasion of Stanley Hauerwas's 70th Birthday,* ed. Charles R. Pinches, Kelly S. Johnson, and Charles M. Collier (Eugene, OR: Cascade, 2010), 26–27.

[12] Elliot, "Christian as Homo Viator," 104–9.

[13] Susannah Ticciati, *Job and the Disruption of Identity: Reading beyond Barth* (London: T&T Clark, 2005), 162–74: "Not to wrestle with God, therefore, would be on Job's part a denial of the truth of his existence" (173).

[14] Ticciati, *Job and the Disruption of Identity,* 167.

[15] Eschatological hope includes, then, a finality where peace and home will be found. Confused roaming will end; exploration will not.

[16] Migrating from the Ur of the Chaldeans, Terah, Abram's father, and his extended family set out for Canaan but settled in Haran (Gen. 11:31–32). Upon Terah's death, God prompted Abram to leave Haran for Canaan.

[17] See Miroslav Volf, *Exclusion and Embrace: A Theological Exploration of Identity, Otherness, and Reconciliation* (Nashville: Abingdon, 1996), 38–40.

[18] McGill, *Religious Identity,* 39–41.

[19] A. N. Williams, "Assimilation and Otherness: The Theological Significance of Négritude," *International Journal of Systematic Theology* 11, no. 3 (2009): 265. Williams elaborates on this relationality within the Trinity, between God and humanity, and between persons. Individuals can choose to shift their definition of self and their identity by taking in some aspect of another and changing the nature of their relationality. A person's identity is changed by one's "determination toward another."

[20] Jeremy Gabrielson, "Paul's Non-Violent Gospel: The Theological Politics of Peace in Paul's Life and Letters" (PhD diss., University of St. Andrews, 2011), 123–29. Gabrielson cites John Barclay that divine and human agency hang in "dialectical fashion" (124), alluding to Hegel's method of dialectics where two apparent or truly contradictory statements are held together, and even resolved, by their interaction.

[21] Klyne Snodgrass, "Paul's Focus on Identity," *Bibliotheca Sacra* 168, no. 671 (July–September 2011): 262–66. He lists eight factors for a hermeneutics of identity: one's physical and psychical makeup, histories, relations, commitments (to location, investments, oppositions, attitudes, activities, icons, and persons), boundaries, being as an ongoing process of change, an internal self-interpreting memory, and one's sense of future. See "Introduction to a Hermeneutics of Identity," *Bibliotheca Sacra* 168, no. 669 (January–March 2011): 3–19.

[22] I am applying McAdams's theory of life-story identity configuration and integration to the Christian. McAdams, "Redemptive Self," 99.

[23] Hauerwas, *Christian Existence*, 39.

[24] Volf treats Gilles Deleuze's consideration of departure as nomadic (namely as without a beginning, destination, particularity, or directing agent) as futile wandering and as unrelated to the Abrahamic example. A further charge against Deleuze's rendering is that his conception does not explain how one can "resist the evildoer." Volf, *Exclusion and Embrace*, 40–41.

[25] Jürgen Moltmann, "Theology in the Project of the Modern World," in *A Passion for God's Reign: Theology, Christian Learning and the Christian Self*, ed. Miroslav Volf (Grand Rapids, MI: Eerdmans, 1998), 31–32.

[26] Miroslav Volf, *The End of Memory: Remembering Rightly in a Violent World* (Grand Rapids, MI: Eerdmans, 2006), 198.

[27] Stanley J. Grenz, "The Social God and the Relational Self: Toward a Theology of the Imago Dei in the Postmodern Context," in *Personal Identity in Theological Perspective*, ed. Richard Lints, Michael S. Horton, and Mark R. Talbot (Grand Rapids, MI: Eerdmans, 2006), 91.

[28] Miroslav Volf, "Being as God Is," in *God's Life in Trinity*, ed. Miroslav Volf and Michael Welker (Minneapolis: Fortress Press, 2006), 1–2.

[29] The idea of the Holy Spirit as chaperone is taken from the sermon of Kevin McGill on Ephesians 1, Fellowship Bible Church, Dallas, October 7, 2007.

[30] Hauerwas and Willimon, *Resident Aliens*, 86–92; Miroslav Volf, *After Our Likeness: The Church as the Image of the Trinity* (Grand Rapids, MI: Eerdmans, 1998), 127–35.

[31] Volf, *Exclusion and Embrace*, 27; Volf, *End of Memory*, 108, 179–80, 199, 202, 207.

[32] One's internalized identity does not prevent the intrusion and presumption of the other to impose an identity on that individual that one would not own. Charles Taylor, "The Politics of Recognition," in *Multiculturalism: Examining the Politics of*

Recognition, ed. Charles Taylor and Amy Gutmann (Princeton: Princeton University Press, 1994), 25–26.

[33] William S. Campbell, *Paul and the Creation of Christian Identity* (London: T&T Clark, 2006), 14.

[34] Stanley Hauerwas, *The Peaceable Kingdom: A Primer in Christian Ethics* (Notre Dame: University of Notre Dame Press, 1983), 150.

[35] Hauerwas and Willimon, *Resident Aliens,* 17–18.

[36] Volf, *Exclusion and Embrace,* 178–80, 189.

[37] Volf speaks of displacement in a different sense—that of self being displaced to let in the divine Other. *End of Memory,* 198.

[38] Clemens Sedmak, *The Capacity to Be Displaced: Resilience, Mission, and Inner Strength* (Boston: Brill, 2017), 6–14.

[39] Sedmak, *The Capacity to Be Displaced,* 10–11, 58–59.

[40] Jehu Hanciles, *Beyond Christendom: Globalization, African Migration, and the Transformation of the West* (Maryknoll, NY: Orbis, 2008), 147.

[41] Volf, *Exclusion and Embrace,* 49–51, 65–68.

Identity as Christian and Cultural
A Case Study of India

ANDREW B. SPURGEON

C an a person be both "an Indian" and "a Christian"? The Hindu nationalists claim Hindus alone are Indians. Rajeshwar Singh, for example, says, "Our target is to make India a Hindu Rashtra [nation] by 2021. The Muslims and Christians don't have any right to stay here. So they would either be converted to Hinduism or forced to run away from [India]."[1] Singh assumes that India has always been a Hindu nation, but ancient Indians were animists; Hinduism came to India between 1800 and 500 BCE. Nevertheless, is being a Hindu a synonym for being an Indian? Must all Indians be Hindus?

To answer these questions, first I will explain what makes a person an Indian. Second, I will answer how a person lives as an Indian Christian.

Being Indian

The government of India issues Indian passports to anyone who can prove at least one parent is an Indian. A passport does not make a person Indian— people with Indian passports live in every nation but have no cultural identity as Indians. Similarly, people from many nations live as Indians in India. Sonia Gandhi, the daughter of Italian parents, married an Indian and has represented Indians as the president of the Indian National Congress since 1998. What, then, makes a person Indian?

Pavan K. Varma lists several "value-neutral" qualities of Indians, such as a desire for power, a hierarchal outlook on life, a hunger for wealth, a tendency for self-absorption, and a leaning toward violence.[2] His assessments may shock readers who, for example, think of India as a nonviolent country. Varma explains:

> In general, Indians are opposed to violence if it creates a
> degree of instability or disorder that threatens the social system.
> However, in a controlled milieu, such as the enforcement of
> caste hierarchy or purity, when violence has social sanction or is
> backed by numerical strength, [Indians] can be as violent as any
> other race.[3]

The violence against Christians in Orissa seems to support Varma's claim.[4]

Sudhir Kakar, a cultural psychologist, outlines "Indian-ness" slightly differently:

> "Indian-ness" is the cultural part of mind that informs the activi-
> ties and concerns of daily life of vast number of Indians. How
> we behave toward superiors and subordinates in organizations,
> the kinds of food conducive of health and vitality, the web of
> duties and obligations in family life, are as much influenced by
> the cultural part of the mind as are ideas on the proper relation-
> ship between the sexes, or the one to the Divine.[5]

Borrowing from Kakar's general outline, I have selected five features of "Indian-ness" that intersect with Christian theology. As an Indian and an observer of my culture, I have chosen India's caste system, belief in polytheism, treatment of women, belief in reincarnation, and *prasada* ("gift of God") as test cases for my exposition that a person can be both an Indian and a Christian.

India's Caste System

Manusmriti, a Hindu sacred text, segregates people into priests (*Brahmins*), warriors (*Kshtriyas*), merchants (*Vysys*), and workers (*Shudras*). It further divides these categories by birth, color, and profession. The people of the lowest caste were allotted to the Scheduled Tribes (*adivasi*) and Scheduled Castes (*dalit*). B. R. Ambedkar, a freedom fighter, explains the association between Hinduism and caste system in seven propositions:

> (1) The people who created [Hinduism] belonged to the Aryan race; (2) This Aryan race came from outside India and invaded India; (3) The native of India were known as Dasas and Dasyus who were radically different from the Aryans; (4) The Aryans were a white race. The Dasas and Dasyus were a dark race; (5) The Aryans conquered the Dasas and Dasyus; (6) The Dasas and Dasyus after they were conquered and enslaved were called Shudras; (7) The Aryans cherished color prejudice and . . . separated the white race from the black race.[6]

Color racism exists worldwide, and most societies shun, at least officially, discrimination based on the color of skin. The Constitution of India, however, upholds caste divisions—evidenced by laws that reclassified the Scheduled Caste.[7]

Indians, in general, follow the caste system. My high school certificate designates me a *Nadar* (landworker) of the *Shudras* caste (the workers). Even today, when Indians seek spouses for their children, they start by asking the potential spouse's caste. Will India ever overcome caste delineation? Time will tell. Regardless, "Indian-ness" involves caste identity.

Belief in Polytheism

Centuries ago (circa 700 BCE), a Hindu student, Yajnavalkya, asked his teacher, Aruni, how many gods were in Hinduism. Aruni replied, "Three hundred and three and three thousand and three." Unsatisfied with the answer, Yajnavalkya pressed Aruni further. The teacher concluded by saying, "There is only one 'God,' the *BRAHMAN*, or all."[8] This statement summarizes Hinduism—it is a monotheistic-polytheistic religion. A Hindu believes in one *Brahman* (god) who appears in many forms. As such, a Hindu has no qualms worshiping one or many gods. Gandhi, when assassinated, called upon the god Rama before he died.[9] Although he was a devoted Hindu, he followed some of the teachings of Jesus Christ.[10]

Similarly, Indians do not consider themselves to be idol worshipers or idolaters. To an untrained outsider (especially a Christian), an idol itself is considered a god, and worshiping an idol is idolatry. But to a Hindu Indian, idols are physical representation of gods but not gods. Gandhi, for example, said, "No Hindu considers an image to be God."[11] An idol, in Hinduism, is a *murti*—a "solid body" representing a spirit god. These *murti* draw veneration and respect from the Hindus, but the *murti* are not gods. A *linga* (genitalia), a Hindu *murti*, does not represent a phallus, immorality, fertility, or infertility; it represents the deity Shiva.[12]

In prayers for health and well-being, Hindu Indians often allocate different responsibilities to different gods. My neighbor once said to me, "I pray to Vishnu for my health, Lakshmi for my wealth, and Ganesh for my children's education. How can you pray to one god and expect him to solve your problems?" For most Indians, monotheism—not polytheism—seems to be an odd faith.

Treatment of Women

"We cry the day a woman is born and the day she is married, but we heave a sigh of relief on the day she dies," said an Indian village woman to a reporter, reflecting on her life experience and the culture's ill treatment of women.[13] Yet India has not always treated women poorly. Indira Gandhi became India's prime minister well before women in Western countries ran for the top offices of their nations. The Hindu Succession Act of June 17, 1956, became the first gender-equitable law in India after the century-long British rule that excluded women from inheritance in rural Punjab . . . [making] provisions for married and unmarried daughters, sisters, widows and mothers to inherit land with full proprietary rights to its disposal.[14]

However, despite these cultural advances, some Indian husbands beat their wives, young men gang rape young women, husbands set their wives on fire for dowry-debt, and some think of *sati*—the practice of widows dying on their husbands' funeral pyres—as a chaste and noble act.[15] Varma lists acts of violence against Indian women:

> On Independence Day, 15 August 2001, 17-year-old Sanju Chauhan was murdered . . . on the suspicion that she had had an affair and had given birth to an illegitimate child. In the same month, Vishal Sharma, 18, and Sonu Singh, 17, were hanged by their families . . . for daring to want an inter-caste marriage. . . . On 9 February 2002, . . . Shobah, a girl of 15 working as a domestic help in the home of a senior government official in New Delhi, . . . had been branded with a hot iron and her hands burnt in hot lentil soup for "disobedience". On 4 July 2003, Ponamma, a 30-year-old widow with AIDS, was allegedly stoned to death by her relatives and neighbors.[16]

It seems Indians love their mothers, their goddesses, and their rulers, but they hate their spouses, servants, widows, and girl children. According to a 1994 report, in one of the hospitals in Madurai, a city in the state of Tamil Nadu, "out of nearly 600 female births, 570 babies vanish every year. Hospital sources estimate more than 450 are female infanticide victims."[17] Crimes against women are not unique to India, yet one wonders if Indians value women, considering their long history of ill treatment.

Belief in Reincarnation
Gandhi once said,

> Men are equal. For, though they are not of the same age, same height, the same skin and the same intellect . . . the soul that is hidden beneath this earthly crust is one and the same for all men and women belonging to all climes.[18]

His principle of equality stemmed from his Hinduism, which sees all of humanity as a single soul. In Hinduism, life never ends; it reincarnates. "There are no common burial grounds in Hinduism because death is not a permanent condition."[19]

With belief in the oneness of the human soul, then, why is there caste delineation, poverty, and the abuse of women? The belief in *karma*—that one's actions in the previous life influence the subsequent life—is the reason. The Hindu scriptures say, "A man who steals gems, pearls, corals, or any of the various precious substances out of greed is born among gold-smiths. . . . By stealing grain, one becomes a rat . . . by stealing a deer or an elephant, a wolf" (*Manuvadharmasastra*, 12.61–67).

Since one's actions in the previous life influence the present life (*karma*), the only way to end *karma* is to "live out" the life the gods have offered, including enduring suffering. Helping a beggar is to disrupt his/her *karma*, which will affect his/her future incarnations. Past, present, and future connect in a person's caste, color, wealth, and gender.

Indians therefore have a unique outlook on poverty, suffering, caste, life, and death. The nation can ignore the deaths of hundreds of female children since their life will reincarnate; those babies, if they suffer well in this life, will reincarnate into a better person, possibly a boy and into a Brahmin caste.

Prasada

Prasada refers to a deity's grace bestowed on worshipers. Hindu worship-ers bring fruit, milk, and coconuts and offer them to their gods. After the gods have had their fill and blessed them, the priests return the deity's grace (*prasada*) to the worshipers. The worshipers either eat the *prasada* in the presence of the gods or take them home to share with their families.

Prasada is a hallmark of "south Asian civilization."[20] A visitor to India will see food offered to gods in restaurants, butcher shops, and grocery stores. These shopkeepers will not offer their services to the public until they have fed their gods and have shared the *prasada* with the priests. When Indians dedicate a building or a bridge, when they buy a car or a cow, when they give birth to or marry off their children, they feed gods and share the blessings, *prasada*, with their neighbors. Seeking the gods' favor and sharing them with one another is another part of being an Indian.

Summary

Although most Indian Christians have rejected these beliefs as part of Hinduism and have isolated themselves from their neighbors (drawing the accusation that Christianity is "a foreign religion"), these cultural beliefs do affect them. Living with 966 million Hindus has its impact on Indian Christians. As such, they have become, in the words of Havilah Dharamraj and Angukali V. Rotokha, "blue jackals":

> The *Panchatantra* [an ancient Indian writing] tells the story of Chandarava the jackal. In his search for food he strayed into the city. Beset by dogs, he fled into a dyer's courtyard and hastily leaped into a vat of indigo dye. Since his new *avatar* defied identification as any known beast, the blue jackal was elevated to kingship over the animals of the forest. He proclaimed himself to be Kukudruma, the heaven-sent. One day, the howling of a pack of passing jackals fell on his indigo ears. Instinctively, he raised his head and howled a response. His cloak of anonymity fell, and so did he. Without pressing the parallels too far, it can be suggested that the Indian Christian is, metaphorically speaking, a blue jackal, in that he is unsure who he is—Chandarava or Kukudruma, or both.[21]

Hindu militants fear that these blue jackals, Indian Christians, will destroy India by abolishing caste distinctions, replacing polytheism with monotheism, elevating women, denying the belief in reincarnation (and help the poor and social outcastes), and ending the multibillion dollar industry of seeking gods' favors (including pilgrimages to the River Ganges). In reality, the blue jackals are not a real threat, since they vacillate between identifying as Christians and what they actually do as Indians. They speak against caste discrimination until they apply for college admission or search for spouses for their children. While opposing polytheism, they fear the evil eye or bad omens and seek auspicious days (days that bring good luck and the gods' favor). Indian Christians profess to abhor violence against women, yet some beat their wives. They speak of eternal life but unlawfully hoard wealth in this life. Without reason, they fear association with their Hindu neighbors and eating their food. With God's grace and their commitment to faith, however, Indian Christians truly can identify as Indians and Christians, which is what I would like to expound in the next section.

Being an Indian Christian

Sundar Singh, a Sikh convert to Christianity a century ago, modeled an Indian Christian lifestyle by living as a Sikh yet believing wholeheartedly in Jesus Christ. He cautioned:

> Indians do need the water of life, but not in a European cup.
> They should sit down on the floor in church; they should take off their shoes instead of their turbans. Indian music should be sung. Long informal addresses should take the place of sermons.[22]

Here, I will address the five characteristics of Indian culture that I discussed earlier to show how Indian Christians can hold both Indian and Christian identities as transformed people (Rom. 12:1–2).

Indian Christians and the Caste System

Since the time the gospel came to India, Indian Christians have struggled to find their role in the caste system. Western missionaries taught them to abandon the caste system, thinking it an evil practice, but they did not realize how caste affects one's family, income, and livelihood. Scholars explain:

> In response to the burden of social stigma and economic backwardness borne by persons belonging to some of India's castes, the Constitution of India allows for special provisions for members of these castes. . . . These special provisions have taken two main forms: action against adverse discrimination towards persons from the SC [Scheduled Caste] and the ST [Scheduled Tribe]; and compensatory discrimination in favor of persons from the SC and the ST. Compensatory discrimination has taken the form of guaranteeing seats in national and state legislatures and in the village *panchayats* [judgment courts], places in educational institutes, and the reservation of a certain proportion of government jobs for the SC and the ST.[23]

The Indian Constitution incorporates caste distinctions to provide "compensatory discrimination" for those in disadvantaged groups (like affirmative action). Asking a new convert to Christianity from a low caste to forsake one's caste would cost one to forsake a place in the educational system, the job market, or in politics. Those who receive regular foreign income (missionaries and Christian leaders) do not understand a poor Indian's dilemma: "Should I declare that I am a Christian and lose my caste identity and the privileges associated with it, or should I remain a Hindu?" The privileged can afford to be casteless, but an Indian farmer cannot. How, then, can Indian Christians work within a caste system?

Apostle Paul gave a principle to a parallel culture, the Corinthians. He wrote, "Though I am free and belong to no one, I have made myself a slave to everyone, to win as many as possible" (1 Cor. 9:19). Paul, a free Roman citizen, chose slavery for the advancement of the gospel. Indian Christians, although casteless in Christ, can tolerate the caste system and use its positive aspects for the advancement of the gospel.

First, Indian Christians can allow converts from the lowest of castes to remain in their caste so that they can retain their jobs and privileges. Studies show that the provision in the Indian Constitution has resulted in a five percent increase "in regular salaried and wage employment" among these groups.[24] Caste is functional, at least, in providing jobs for the poor. Allowing a *dalit* (low caste member) to keep his or her caste and enjoy the benefits will only progress the gospel.

Second, Indian Christians who retain their caste identity can enter India's legal (*panchayats*) and political systems and defend Christianity. Charan Banerjee (1847–1902), a Hindu convert from Bengal, joined the Indian National Congress in 1885 and defended Bengali Christians as Indians. "In having become Christians, we have not ceased to be Hindus. We are Hindu Christians. . . . We have embraced Christianity but we have not discarded our nationality."[25] Brahmabadhav Upadhyay, another convert to Christianity, fought for India's independence through his writing in both Bengali and English.[26] Christians, by retaining their caste identities, can enter India's legal and political arena under the Constitution and defend Christianity as an Indian faith.

Third, Indian Christians should not commit any caste discrimination but should fight against the evils of the caste system. Paul, who subjected himself to slavery for the advancement of the gospel, fought against the evils of slavery. He wrote to the Corinthians, "If you can gain your freedom, do so" (1 Cor. 7:21). He then pleaded with his friend, Philemon, for the freedom of Onesimus, a slave (Philem. 1:8–16). Unfortunately, some Indian Christians practice the evils of the caste system. Paul Bubash writes, "Rev. A. Maria Arul Raja, a Catholic priest and a director of the theology PhD program in Delhi, cannot talk to his bishop more than five minutes. . . . Why? He was born a Dalit, a member of the untouchable caste."[27] While utilizing the positive aspects of the caste system for the betterment of the poor, Indian Christians should not practice its evils. Indian Christians are not casteless, but they should be caste opportunists—those who use the constitutional privileges of the caste system to uplift people and further the gospel. At the same time, they should also fight against social inequalities and the abuse of the low caste.

Indian Christians and Polytheism

No other contemporary culture resembles the polytheism of the Greco-Roman culture like India's culture. Just as pantheons of gods and goddesses governed the lives of the Romans, they govern the lives of the Indians. Interestingly, as referenced previously, Hinduism is a monotheistic polytheism. Suhag Shukla, the founder of the Hindu American Foundation, says the number-one myth about Hinduism is saying that Hindus worship 330 million gods. She writes, "There is one supreme God that cannot be fully known or understood. Hindus are encouraged to relate to God in the way that suits them best, like worshiping many deities who are believed to be manifestations of God. . . . That's why Hinduism is often thought of as polytheistic. It is not."[28] In other words, Hindus worship one god through various *avatars* (personifications, manifestations).

Since each *avatar* has a specific responsibility, a Hindu worshiper addresses various *avatars* at multiple times a day in the form of *pujas*:

> Strictly speaking, a *puja* is a formal mode of worship with
> conventionally prescribed procedures. . . . The procedures are
> usually about fourteen or sixteen in number. Among the impor-
> tant procedures of a *puja* are the initial invocation of the Lord
> (*avahana*), the invitation to a seat (*asana*), the washing of the
> feet (*padya*), the offering of flowers (*pushpa*), the waving of

lights (*dipa*), and the consecration of food (*naivedya*). These acts are accompanied by the recitation of appropriate scriptural texts and meditation.[29]

A Hindu who performs fourteen to sixteen steps of *puja* daily to multiple gods and goddesses finds Christians to be irreligious and impious. How can Indian Christians relate to such a pious culture?

First, Indian Christians should not advance the oft-repeated claim that Hindus worship millions of gods. This angers the Hindus and hinders the advancement of the gospel. Paul, in Athens, said, "People of Athens! I see that in every way you are very religious" (Acts 17:22). Paul did not condemn the Athenians as polytheists; he exalted them as "very religious." Then he introduced YHWH to them (v. 23). Indians, like the Athenians, are a very religious people, and their polytheism is an expression of their piety. Indian Christians need to present the gospel within the context of piety and without insulting Hindus as polytheists.

Second, Indian Christians need to believe in the existence of other gods and lords. Paul wrote, "For even if there are so-called gods, whether in heaven or on earth (as indeed there are many "gods" and many "lords"), yet for us there is but one God" (1 Cor. 8:5–6). Paul, without denying the existence of other gods, affirms that, for Christians, there is only one God and one Lord. Similarly, Indian Christians can affirm that there are other deities (benevolent or destructive) behind Hindu *avatars*. The task of Indian Christians is not to attack these gods but to approach the worshipers of these deities in gentleness. Once God opens their eyes, they will worship the one true God and Lord (1 Cor. 8:6).

Indian Christians need to find a middle ground between synchronistic theology and Christian militancy. Synchronistic theology teaches that a Hindu can worship YHWH in addition to other gods/goddesses; Christian militancy judges those who disagree with orthodoxy as heretics. A middle ground focuses on the message of Jesus Christ alone. E. Stanley Jones, a missionary to India, said it well:

> If we present Christianity as a rival to other religions, it will fail. Our position should be: There are many religions. There is but one gospel. We are not setting a religion over against other

religions, but a gospel over against human need, which is the same everywhere. The greatest service we can give to anyone in East or West is to introduce him to the moral and spiritual power found in Christ. India needs everything. We humbly offer the best we have. The best we have is Christ.[30]

Indian Christians and Womanhood

A person's religious views influence her understanding of gender. *Mahabharata*, a Hindu scripture, says that the gods, fearing men might become powerful, conquer the world, and dethrone gods, approached the supreme god Brahman for a solution. Brahman created women who, with sexual lusts, ensnared and weakened men, thus averting the dethronement of gods (*Mahab.* 36). The same scripture portrays women as the cause of desire, anger, and death (*Mahab.* 40). With such descriptions of women, no wonder Indians have a love-hate relationship with them.

In response to a protest over the gang rape of a young Indian woman, Urvashi Butalia writes, "Tragically, it takes a case like this to awaken public consciousness, to make people realize that rape and sexual assault are not merely 'women's issues,' they're a symbol of the deep-seated violence that women . . . experience every day in our society."[31] How should Indian Christians live within this context, which is fraught with dangers for women?

First, Indian Christians must believe that when God created people in his image, he created them as "male and female" (Gen. 1:27). Eve was Adam's "bone of [his] bone and flesh of [his] flesh; she shall be called 'woman,' for she was taken out of man" (Gen. 2:23). A biblical view of womanhood is never pejorative. The fifth commandment illustrates this: "Honor your father and your mother, so that you may live long in the land the LORD your God is giving you" (Exod. 20:12; Prov. 1:8). Indian Christians must see women as equal to men.

Second, Indian Christians must shun all malevolent symbols of deep-seated violence against women. When *sati* was frequently practiced in India, William Carey, a Christian missionary, joined the Indian socioreligious reformer Mohan Roy and convinced the governor, Lord William Bentinck, to declare *sati* illegal and criminal. Carey also fought against "polygamy, female infanticide, child marriage, euthanasia, and forced female illiteracy."[32] Christians are not alone in their defense of women. Bhupinder Singh Hooda, the Chief Minister of Haryana, declared the year 2006 to be the Year of the Girl Child and offered "Rs 5000 [$100] per year for five years on the birth of a second daughter in a family."[33] Indian Christians can join such leaders, Christians or Hindus, to promote an esteemed value of womanhood.

Indian Christians and Reincarnation

Hypothetically, a person may escape accountability for the crimes done in this life in two ways. First, if there is no resurrection, whatever crimes one commits will go unpunished, since life will cease at death. Second, if reincarnation is real, the crimes one commits will pass on in the next life to whatever life-form inherits that soul. The absence of resurrection or the presence of reincarnation excuses a person from being accountable in this lifetime.

Christian faith, however, affirms that there is resurrection (1 Cor. 15:12–34), and there is no reincarnation (Heb. 9:27). Believing these doctrines separates Christians from people of other faiths who either deny resurrection or affirm reincarnation. How, then, should an Indian Christian live in a culture that affirms reincarnation?

First, Indian Christians must acknowledge that "the soul that is hidden beneath this earthly crust is one and the same for all men and women,"[34] in the sense that God created all of humanity, including Hindus, in God's image (Gen. 1:26–27). Such an assurance will help Christians overcome their prejudices and reach their neighbors with the gospel.

Second, Indian Christians can equate sin with *karma*, meaning that actions have consequence and punishment, but in this life. Hindus who follow between fourteen and sixteen steps of *puja* to please their gods find Christians, who claim that God has forgiven them and their lack of piety, incomprehensible. But if they see that Christians take sin seriously (Rom. 2:6–8) and worship piously, maybe they will be drawn to Christian faith. Herbert Hoefer writes, "Spiritual authenticity is the critical issue in the Indian mentality. It's the issue that lies behind the guru-principle in Hinduism."[35] If Indian Christians enter their church building all through the day and pray frequently, maybe pious Hindus, who visit their temples several times a day, will see Indian Christians as pious and take the faith of Christians more seriously.

Indian Christians and Prasada

In Hindu culture, one's piety is closely connected to eating *prasada*. Rambachan explains, "The *puja* ritual concludes with the distribution of *prasada*, food which has been ritually offered to the deity. The acceptance of *prasada* is an acknowledgement of the Lord as the source of all that we enjoy."[36] Hindus love to share *prasada* food with their neighbors. But early Christian missionaries, without understanding Indian culture, taught Indian Christians to avoid *prasada*. As a result, Indian Christians have refused Hindu neighbors' *prasada* and isolated themselves from the Indian community.

Indian Christians need to reevaluate the Bible's teachings on food offered to idols. Paul addressed that topic in 1 Corinthians 8–10.[37] Although he prohibited a Christian from entering a temple to eat food offered to a god, since it might lead a weak Christian to idolatry (1 Cor. 8:1–10:24), he permitted Christians in Corinth to eat any food offered in the market, even food that had been offered to a god before it was sold in the market (1 Cor. 10:25–26), and any food offered by a non-Christian (v. 27–31). Paul's guiding principles were, "The earth is the Lord's, and everything in it" (v. 26), and "If I take part in the meal with thankfulness, why am I denounced because of something I thank God for?" (v. 30). These passages help Indian Christians understand how to respond to *prasada* offered to them by Hindus.

First, Indian Christians should not actively seek *prasada* or enter other gods' temples to eat them. Some radical Indian Christians have been known to enter Sikh and Hindu temples to eat free food, *prasada*. Their actions confuse the Hindus; while these Christians claim that they worship a jealous God who abhors idolaters, they seek out *prasada*. Instead of confusing the Hindus, Indian Christians should follow Paul's example: "If what I eat causes anyone to fall into sin, I will never eat meat again, so that I will not cause them to fall" (1 Cor. 8:13). Going hungry is better than free food in a temple.

Second, when neighbors offer *prasada*, Christians should accept if they are being watched and expected to eat it with them. They should eat the *prasada* with thanksgiving (1 Cor. 10: 26, 30). Christians should operate on the principle that "[w]hether [they] eat or drink or whatever [they] do, do it all for the glory of God" (1 Cor. 10:31). If by eating *prasada* they lead someone to idolatry, they should not eat it; their eating will not glorify God. If by eating *prasada* they draw someone to Christ, they should eat it; that kind gesture of accepting a gift from a nonbeliever will glorify God.

Conclusion

When my colleague Dave Raj accepted Christ as his Lord and left the Hindu faith, his Hindu family thought he had forsaken his Indian-ness. He later married a Christian woman, which caused his family to abandon any hope of him returning to Hinduism. When Dave Raj announced that his wife was pregnant, his family wanted to celebrate the life but were hesitant because they worried the baby would have a Western name. Dave Raj surprised his Hindu family and affirmed his Indian-ness by naming his son Arun Raj.

Indian Christians can be fully Christian and fully Indian. Yet some have not been successful in maintaining both identities; they often have been blue jackals—confused by their own identity. But it is not too late. Even as Hindu militants claim that Christians cannot be Indians, Indian Christians can prove they are both. It is a difficult path, but others have walked it. And by walking on it, Indian Christians will draw more Indians to Christ by offering his living water in native cups (John 4:14; 7:37–39).

NOTES

[1] Piyush Srivastava, "'We Will Free India of Muslims and Christians by 2021': DJS Leader Vows to Continue 'Ghar Wapsi' Plans and Restore 'Hindu Glory,'" *Daily Mail*, December 18, 2014, http://www.dailymail.co.uk/indiahome/indianews/article-2879597 /We-free-India-Muslims-Christians-2021-DJS-leader-vows-continue-ghar-wapsi -plans-restore-Hindu-glory.html.

[2] Pavan K. Varma, *Being Indian: Inside the Real India* (London: Arrow Books, 2006), 6–7.

[3] Varma, *Being Indian*, 8.

[4] For the horrors, see Pralay Kanungo, "Hindutva's Fury against Christians in Orissa," *Economics & Political Weekly* 43, no. 37 (2008): 16.

[5] Sudhir Kakar, "Indian-ness: So What Really Makes Indians Indian?," *Little India*, April 2, 2007, https://littleindia.com/indian-ness/

[6] B. R. Ambedkar, "Who Were the Shudras?," in *Babasaheb Ambedkar: Writings and Speeches*, ed. Vasant Moon (Bombay: Education Department, Government of Maharastra, 1990), 57–58.

[7] "Cabinet Approves Amendments in Constitution (Scheduled Castes) Order, 1950," *Sify News*, February 1, 2017. http://www.sify.com/news/cabinet-approves-amendments -in-constitution-scheduled-castes-orders-news-national-rcbnL5fajbeee.html.

[8] Constance A. Jones and James D. Ryan, *Encyclopedia of Hinduism*, Encyclopedia of World Religions (New York: Facts on File, 2007), 507.

[9] "Hey Ram Were Gandhi's Last Words, Says Grandson," *The Times of India*, February 1, 2006. https://timesofindia.indiatimes.com/india/Hey-Ram-were-Gandhis -last-words-says-grandson/articleshow/1395570.cms.

[10] S. K. George, *Gandhi's Challenge to Christianity* (Ahmedabad, India: Navajivan Publishing House, 1947), 8.

[11] Charles R. Andrews, *Mahatma Gandhi: His Life and Ideas* (Delhi: Jaico Publishing House, 2005), 12.

[12] Anantanand Rambachan, "Seeing the Divine in All Forms: The Culmination of Hindu Worship," *Dialogue & Alliance* 4, no. 1 (1990): 6.

[13] Vanaja Dhruvarajan, *Hindu Women and the Power of Ideology* (Granby, MA: Bergin & Garvey, 1989), 96.

[14] Vandana Shukla, "Hindu Women and Property: Myth vs. Reality," *The Tribune*, September 12, 2015, http://www.tribuneindia.com/news/comment/hindu-women -property-myth-vs-reality/131896.html.

[15] Glenn E. Yocum, "Burning 'Widows,' Sacred 'Prostitutes,' and 'Perfect Wives': Recent Studies of Hindu Women," *Religious Studies Review* 20, no. 4 (1994): 277–85. *Sati*, although abolished in theory, still happens, as news media televises it. See "Roop Committed Sati of Her Own Free Will," *The Indian Post*, December 15, 1988, 5.

[16] Varma, *Being Indian*, 149–50.

[17] "Girls in India Marked for Death," *The Christian Century* 112, no. 10 (March 22, 1995): 324.

[18] Mohandas K. Gandhi, *None High, None Low* (Bombay: Bharatiya Vidya Bhavan, 1975), 2.

[19] Knut A. Jacobsen, "Three Functions of Hell in the Hindu Traditions," *Numen* 56, no. 2–3 (2009): 385–86.

[20]Andrea Marion Pinkney, "Prasāda, the Gracious Gift, in Contemporary and Classical South Asia," *Journal of the American Academy of Religion* 81, no. 3 (2013): 735.

[21]Havilah Dharamraj and Angukali V. Rotokha, "History, History Books and the Blue Jackal," in *Indian and Christian: Changing Identities in Modern India, Papers from the First Saiacs Annual Consultation*, ed. Cornelis Bennema and Paul Joshua Bhakiaraj (Bangalore, India: SAIACS Press, 2011), 14.

[22]Burnett Hillman Streeter and Aiyadurai Jesudasen Appasamy, *The Sadhu: A Study in Mysticism and Practical Religion* (London: Macmillan, 1921), 228.

[23]Vani K. Borooah, Amaresh Dubey, and Sriya Iyer, "The Effectiveness of Jobs Reservation: Caste, Religion and Economic Status in India," *Development and Change* 38, no. 3 (2007): 423–24.

[24]Borooah, Dubey, and Iyer, "The Effectiveness of Jobs Reservation," 443.

[25]Kay Baago, *A History of the National Christian Council of India, 1914–1964* (Nagpur, India: The National Christian Council, 1967), 67.

[26]Julius Lipner and George Gispert-Sauch, eds., *The Writings of Brahmabandhab Upadhyay: Including a Resumé of His Life and Thought*, 2 vols. (Bangalore, India: United Theological College, 1991).

[27]Paul Bubash, "Dalit Theology and Spiritual Oppression: A Call to Holiness in a Universal Church," *Journal of Theta Alpha Kappa* 38, no. 2 (2014): 36–37.

[28]Moni Basu, "9 Myths about Hinduism—Debunked," *CNN Belief Blog*, April 25, 2014, http://religion.blogs.cnn.com/2014/04/25/9-myths-about-hinduism-debunked /comment-page-1/.

[29]Rambachan, "Seeing the Divine in All Forms: The Culmination of Hindu Worship," 9.

[30]E. Stanley Jones, "Report on the New India," *The Christian Century* 64, no. 18 (1947): 556.

[31]Urvashi Butalia, "Let's Ask How We Contribute to Rape," *The Hindu*, December 25, 2012, http://www.thehindu.com/opinion/op-ed/lets-ask-how-we-contribute-to-rape /article4235902.ece.

[32]Dibin Samuel, "Wiliam Carey Played Significant Role in Abolishing Sati System," *Christian Today*, December 4, 2009, http://www.christiantoday.co.in/article/wiliam .carey.played.significant.role.in.abolishing.sati.system/4906.htm.

[33]*A Girl's Right to Live: Female Foeticide and Girl Infanticide* (Geneva: NGO Committee on the Status of Women, 2007): 18, https://wilpf.org/wp-content /uploads/2014/07/2007_A_Girls_Right_to_Live.pdf.

[34]Gandhi, *None High, None Low*, 2.

[35]Herbert E. Hoefer, *Churchless Christianity* (Madras, India: Asian Program for Advancement of Training and Studies India, 1991), 36.

[36]Rambachan, "Seeing the Divine in All Forms: The Culmination of Hindu Worship," 9.

[37]For a detailed study, see Andrew B. Spurgeon, *Twin Cultures Separated by Centuries: An Indian Reading of 1 Corinthians* (Carlisle, UK: Langham Global Library, 2016).

Christian Identity and Embodied Being
Toward Valuing Our Bodies

LISA IGRAM

I serve as an associate dean of spiritual development at a faith-based university in California. My work revolves around conversations with emerging adults (eighteen to twenty-four years old) who wrestle with a variety of life and faith questions. I listen to students who desperately seek to be in the center of God's will—of finding that one "right" internship or person to marry or career path to follow. I listen to stories of overcommitment and exhaustion from students who care deeply about serving God and find themselves saying "yes" to all kinds of good things to the detriment of their emotional and physical health. I listen to frustrations over patterns of sin that echo Paul's lament, "I don't understand: what I want to do I do not do, but what I hate I do" (Rom. 7:15, author's paraphrase). I listen to students using rather individualistic "Jesus and me" language as they talk about how they need to depend more on God and less on family or friends—a decision that often coincides with relational struggles that are too difficult to face.

As I listen, I have begun to wonder how much of these young people's struggles to know God's will and to do the "right thing" is undergirded by an overly spiritualized faith that has divorced our spirituality from our very real existence as physical, embodied beings. Their instinct to focus on their spiritual lives with little regard for their physical bodies makes sense. Western spirituality has long been guided by the notion of preparing the soul for eternity. From ancient ascetic practices, to revival era talk of "saving souls," to my students' focus on personal "quiet times" of prayer and Scripture reading, the soul's formation is the focus of discipleship, and in my university context, spiritual growth is fostered through the development of the mind. Western theology holds within its deepest assumptions varying shades of soul/body or mind/body dualism that privilege the value of the soul or mind over the body. No wonder I hear this bias when some of my students talk about their deepest struggles.

Over the last century, however, advances in neuroscience as well as philosophical paradigm shifts have brought into question the fundamental assumption that the mind or soul ought to be privileged above the body, and these questions have created space to reconsider the value of embodiment in the theology and practices of Christian formation. In the next few pages, I will explore contemporary and historical conversations around the mind/body divide, including what biblical authors may have assumed about each, and will suggest implications for a more robust spirituality that values the identity of persons as embodied beings.

The Mind-Body Problem in Current Philosophical and Theological Scholarship

Prompted by scientific discoveries within the last few decades, theological scholarship has revisited the question of mind/body dualism (and the occasional mind/soul/body trichotomism) that has dominated Christian thought and practice, particularly since the Enlightenment. A variety of views on the metaphysical constitution of the human person emerge from these questions and center on whether the human person consists of physical, spiritual, or mental substance, or some combination therein, and how these substances interact. The orthodox views avoid, on the one hand, reductive physical monism that posits human identity as sentient physical matter and, on the other, a Cartesian substance dualism in which human identity is centered on an intellectual consciousness that is only incidentally related to a physical body.[1] Between these extremes lie a variety of views on the metaphysical makeup of humans, three of which will be briefly described here to offer a sense of the nuance and complexity of the mind/body problem: nonreductive physicalism (Joel Green, Nancey Murphy), emergent dualism (William Hasker, Christian Smith), and substance dualism (J. P. Moreland, Scott Rae).

Figure 7.1. Continuum of select metaphysical theories of human anthropology

Motivated in part by a desire to reconcile modern scientific advances with scriptural revelation, theologians such as Joel Green and Nancey Murphy suggest that nonreductive physical monism—the conception of a human as an entirely physical being with the capacity for personhood—is thoroughly compatible with a biblical worldview and may have been assumed by biblical authors.[2] Unlike reductive physicalism, nonreductive physicalism does not see the human person as simply a cluster of physical organs that form a sentient physical body.[3] Instead, nonreductive physical monists draw upon the theory of emergence, which states that the whole is different from the sum of its parts. The physical substance of our bodies gives rise to capacities for reason, rationality, and self-concept—in short, for personhood.[4] Just as water's property of wetness is both different from its constituent parts of two hydrogen atoms and one oxygen atom and cannot be reduced to hydrogen and oxygen while maintaining the wetness of water, so the human being is both different from the sum of his or her physical parts and cannot be reduced to his or her physical parts while maintaining the personhood of a human being. The physical substance of the human body gives rise to emergent capacities that make one a human person.

The views of emergent dualists such as philosopher William Hasker and sociologist Christian Smith overlap in part with the nonreductive physicalist use of emergence theory. Both Hasker and Smith, however, attribute more power to the emergent properties of the body than nonreductive physicalists. Not only is the whole different from the sum of its parts, but the whole also has the capacity to direct its individual parts. The capacity of consciousness that emerges from the brain has the power to direct the functioning of the brain, creating a duality of mind and body: when I become stressed, I can breathe deeply to calm myself; when my hand feels the stove's heat, I can consciously withdraw it to avoid being burned. Hasker also places an emphasis on the teleonomic, or purpose-filled, ends for which God created humanity and asserts that since God "chose to make humans and other sentient creatures out of the dust of the earth, we may well suppose that this Being had the foresight to endow that dust with powers that would enable such a creation."[5] For Hasker and Smith, emergence and substance dualism, where "substance" is emergent and irreducible, go hand in hand.

J. P. Moreland and Scott Rae draw on a Thomistic paradigm of anthropology, which is based on Aristotle's views of essence and form, to articulate a theory of substance dualism that emphasizes the existence of a substance called the "soul." Moreland and Rae argue that God created the soul (the self or "I" that contains the faculty of the mind) as a spiritual substance (essence) that exists in the physical form of the body. While the soul can exist without the physical body, the body is not a body without the soul; it is a corpse.[6] They describe the soul as "an individuated essence that makes the body a human body and that diffuses, informs, animates, develops, unifies, and grounds the biological functions of its body."[7] The human person is a spiritual being necessarily manifest in the physical world through the body.

What Biblical Writers Thought

In their efforts to reconcile scientific scholarship with the biblical account, nonreductive physicalists such as Murphy and Green question dualist readings of the biblical text, which have traditionally assumed the existence of a substantive soul. They suggest that the concept of a soul/body divide was imported from Greek and Roman philosophy, along with a tendency to privilege the soul's spiritual nature over the body's physical nature.[8] Such thinking was then firmly embedded into the post-Enlightenment consciousness through Descartes's famous *cogito ergo sum* ("I think, therefore I am"), which replaced the "soul" with the "mind" and reinforced a hard distinction between mind and body.[9] While each scholar noted thus far would agree that Cartesian dualism unnecessarily reduces personhood to rational consciousness, and even Thomist substance dualists would add that Cartesian dualism too strictly divides mind and body, this idea of a strict mind/body divide endures in the American evangelical imagination and influences how we think about the Christian life. We may be guilty of imposing Cartesian dualism, with its implicit devaluing of the human body, onto Scripture's use of soul, spirit, body, and flesh language in ways that even Moreland and Rae would consider unhelpful.

In some ways, discussions of anthropology within the context of scriptural teaching remains at an impasse: discovering what biblical writers actually thought about humanity's makeup proves challenging, largely due to the reality that New Testament writers lived in a cultural milieu that was influenced not only by the Jewish Torah, Talmud, and *midrashim*, but also by Greek and Roman thought. Generally, Hebrew thought tended toward an aspectival view of the human person, while Greek thought tended to be more partitive.[10] The Hebrew conception of the human person was holistic and used terms such as *nephesh* (נֶפֶשׁ), which referred to spiritual aspects of a human being,[11] and *basar* (בָּשָׂר), which referred to the physical aspects of a human being;[12] each referenced not as separate, joined substances but as an ontological whole to be viewed from a different perspective or aspect.[13] It might seem reasonable to assume, for example, that Paul, as a Jew, had a Hebrew understanding of humanity. During the writing of the New Testament canon, however, Greek and Roman popular philosophical thought influenced the development of both Jewish and Christian theology and practice.

While tending to view the human person more partitively, Greek and Roman philosophy held varying understandings of anthropology that ranged from a Platonic soul/body dualism, which emphasized the immortality and superiority of the soul, to the monist physicalism of Epicurean philosophy, which taught that this physical life is all there is (so "eat, drink, and be merry, for tomorrow we die!").[14] At times, it seems that a dualism or even a trichotomism of some kind influenced Paul, as he references the mind (νοῦς, *nous*), spirit (πνεῦμα, *pneuma*) or soul (ψυχή, *psyche*), and body (σῶμα, *soma*) or flesh (σάρξ, *sarx*; e.g., Rom. 8:10; 1 Cor. 2:11; 14:14; Phil. 2:2; 1 Thess. 5:23). Paul's choice of words, however, might reflect a strategy of cultural accommodation. Paul's letters, which have missional and pastoral goals, address his Gentile contemporaries on their terms in his efforts to share the gospel and enculturate new communities into the way of Jesus.[15] Nowhere in his writings does Paul articulate a cohesive theological anthropology—this was not his goal.

More on How We Got Here

The influence of dualism is more clearly evident in early church writings than in the New Testament. On questions of ethics, much ancient thought reflected a dichotomy between reason (associated with the mind or soul) and passion (associated with the body), in which the reasonable mind was charged with overcoming the passions of the body for right and proper living. This privileging of reason over passion is evident in the writings of leading theologians over the next several centuries. The highly influential Philo, for example, used Platonic thought to articulate a system of ethics that looked toward escaping the temptations of the physical body.[16] Augustine did the same when he identified the soul as one's essential identity, even as he emphasized the functional unity of the soul and body.[17] As an Aristotelian, Aquinas emphasized a similar functional unity but stressed that imaging God happened through the mind and intellect.[18] In the midst of these discussions, then, existed a subtle yet unmistakable assumption that the soul (or intellect) is paramount, and that part of its function is to discipline the body. Thus a hierarchy developed, for some explicitly and others implicitly: the soul or mind outranked the body in terms of what was most pure and closest to God. By the time Descartes's *cogito* and the Enlightenment arrived, the idea of the soul had been reduced to the intellect, the emphasis of human identity had become its rationality, and in our post-Enlightenment context, the body has been diminished in theological importance and Christian praxis.

In a knowing response to Cartesian dualism's influence on Western culture to conceive of the person as what James K. A. Smith calls "brains on a stick,"[19] many contemporary mind/body theorists now articulate their views with an eye to revaluing the body. Whether asserting that person-hood arises entirely from physical structures or noting that the body is not a body without the God-created soul, each of these theories elevates the value of the body, and even substance dualist J. P. Moreland views a person as a "functional unity" of soul and body.[20] It may be time to overemphasize the value of the body in order to push back against the Enlightenment-influenced divorce between the soul/mind and body that tempts us to dismiss the body altogether. We may even find help from Paul in this endeavor.

Paul on Σῶμα and Σάρξ

While it remains for biblical scholars and philosophers to continue pars-ing out Paul's thoughts on the metaphysical makeup of the human being, clarity may be gained on the theological importance of the body through a deeper understanding of Paul's two primary words to describe it: σῶμα (*soma*, body) and σάρξ (*sarx*, flesh). Consider, for example, the follow-ing verses:

> But if Christ is in you, then even though your body (σῶμα) is subject to death because of sin, the Spirit gives life because of righteousness. (Rom. 8:10)

> For the flesh (σάρξ) desires what is contrary to the Spirit, and the Spirit what is contrary to the flesh (σάρξ). They are in conflict with each other, so that you do not do what you want. (Gal. 5:17)

> The acts of the flesh (σάρξ) are obvious: sexual immorality, impurity, and debauchery. . . . But the fruit of the Spirit is love, joy, peace, patience, kindness, goodness, faithfulness, gentle-ness, and self-control. (Gal. 5:19, 22–23)

If these verses are read with the Cartesian-colored lenses that often accom-pany American evangelicalism, we might assume that Paul viewed the body with great suspicion. We might read the words "flesh" and "body" and picture the physical body's opposition to the soul; we might read "Spirit" and imagine help for our souls as we fight the sin of our physical bodies. In so doing we reinforce Cartesian dualism and the platonic (almost Gnostic) ideal that the goal of the spiritual life is to rid oneself of the shell of the mortal body.

Biblical scholars see otherwise. In his comprehensive work on Paul's use of σῶμα and σάρξ, Robinson writes, "in essence, σάρξ and σῶμα designate different aspects of human relationship to God. While σάρξ stands for man, in the solidarity of creation, in his distance from God, σῶμα stands for man, in the solidarity of creation, as made for God."[21] In *The Mind of the Spirit*, Keener uses carefully chosen phrases to clarify Paul's understanding of the human condition not in terms of substances (flesh, mind, spirit), but rather of two orientations or mind-sets, using Paul's difficult-to-translate φρόνημα (*phronema*, mind-set), derived from φρονέω (*phroneo*, to think, set one's mind on).[22] In discussing the human condition, Paul highlights warring mind-sets—the mind-set of the flesh (σάρξ, *sarx*) as oriented around the world and sinful systems, which leads to death, and the mind-set of the Spirit as oriented around the things of God, which leads to life (Rom. 8:5).[23] Rather than revealing a preference for the immaterial soul over the physical body, Paul seeks to correct the orientation of the mind.

A deeper and more profound undertone is embedded in Paul's use of σῶμα (*soma*, body). Paul most often uses σῶμα in relational contexts (1) to describe the ways Christians in community ought to treat each other (1 Cor. 6:13–18; Eph. 4–5; Phil. 1:24; Col. 2:23; 1 Thess. 4:4), (2) to function as a metaphor for the church (Rom. 12; 1 Cor. 12; Eph. 3:6; Col. 1–2; Col. 3:15), and (3) to illustrate human communion with Christ (Gal. 2:20; 1 Cor. 7:34; 10:16; 11:24–29). Robinson notes that "σῶμα is the nearest equivalent to our word 'personality' . . . [it] is what ties men up with each other, rather than what separates them as individuals."[24] Bultmann sees σῶμα as "man who is in relationship to himself,"[25] and Berger and Betz rightly expand Bultmann's primarily existential reading to include communion with Christ and membership in the church.[26] Dunn writes that Paul's anthropology is marked by casting persons as social beings in relationship with God and God's world. He proposes that σῶμα be translated as "embodiment" rather than "body" to get at the complexity of the term—a complexity that is steeped in relationality.[27] Malina adds, "our first-century person would perceive himself as a distinctive whole set in relation to other such wholes and set within a given social and natural background."[28] This mirrors philosopher Maurice Merleau-Ponty's definition of embodiment, which casts the body not as something we have (a mere physical object) but as something we are ("tied to a certain world" and embedded within a culture and a context).[29] Our identities and our personhood—which are defined by relationships, cultural context, and particular historical place—are wrapped up in our physical bodies.

The ancient church seemed to understand Paul's meaning in ways that we late moderns may have missed. In her study on the ancient and medieval church's understanding of the body, Margaret Bynum writes that, rather than denigrating the physical body, the popular Christian consciousness of the time viewed the body as the person—one's identity was wrapped up in one's embodiment. This belief undergirds the practice of honoring relics (Thomas's finger, for example, was not just a finger, but contained the essence of Thomas himself), as well as elaborate theories on how physical, embodied resurrection might take place:

> Despite its suspicion of flesh and lust, Western Christianity did
> not hate or discount the body. Indeed, person was not person
> without body, and body was the carrier or the expression
> (although the two are not the same thing) of what we today call
> individuality.[30]

Modernity, writes Luke Timothy Johnson, has trained us to emphasize the individual's body, to consider it from a purely physical perspective, and to view it as a problem to be solved; this approach propagates a form of alienation and individualism.[31] Pauline theology, however, uses σῶμα relationally—that is, our embodiment's primary function is for relationship with God, others, and the world.

Embodiment's Primary Function: Relationality

Interestingly, this is not purely a theological concept; the idea that embodiment is deeply wedded to relationality appears in studies across multiple scientific disciplines, including the social sciences. Although modernity has led us into the mind/body dichotomy of pursuing either hyper-rational thought or mindless individual passions ("Just do it!"; "You do you!"), the gifts of modernity's empirical, scientific evidence prove contrary to its very underpinnings. Interpersonal neurobiologist Dan Siegel, who studies the impact of relationships on brain development and neuroplasticity, notes that "the mind develops at the interface of neurophysiological processes and interpersonal relationships," which are mediated by embodiment.[32] Attachment theory states that human personality and identity forms through a child's engagement with early caregivers, and studies reveal that infants are predisposed to imitate other human beings through processes such as neural mirroring, which lead to the development of empathy and the human ability to infer the mental state of others.[33] The cognitive sciences increasingly view the body as shaping the mind.[34] Philosophers discussing cognitive metaphor theory posit that language flows from embodiment. For example, we describe the experience of intimacy as "closeness" and "warmth" because, as infants, we conflate physical closeness to warm-bodied caregivers with the concept of intimate connection; we talk about progress using body-based metaphors like "moving forward" or "gaining ground."[35] The social scientific studies of religion have begun to consider the body as "both a biological and a cultural product, simultaneously physical and symbolic."[36]

Data from multiple disciplines suggest that we are not "brains on a stick." Paul's use of σῶμα and empirically driven studies over the last several decades indicate that a primary function of our embodiment is relationality. The repercussions of a robust understanding of our identity as embodied, and therefore relational, are extensive and reach far beyond the scope of this exploration. It may be interesting to consider, however, what has been assumed to be the mind's primary function—knowledge—through the lens of our embodiment, to begin teasing out possible implications.

Embodied Knowledge as Wisdom

In a post-Enlightenment context shadowed by Descartes's *cogito*, knowledge is cast as entirely intellectual, cognitive, rational, and individual, and truth is cast as propositional. How might our epistemology, our understanding of knowledge and truth, expand if we begin with the assumption that we are embodied beings rather than disembodied minds? The primary metaphor for our Western idea of knowledge is wrapped up in a single aspect of our embodiment: vision ("I see!"; "It's becoming clear!").[37] What if the whole of our embodied senses was involved in knowing, and knowledge and truth were cast in light of relationship with God, others, and the world? Our entire conception of knowledge and truth might shift; knowledge might become less about propositional truth held in the mind and instead gain consequence in embodied physicality of relationship. Knowledge and truth may become, perhaps, something more like discernment and wisdom.

Michael Polanyi was a scientist and philosopher during what was then called the Great War. Born in Bulgaria and eventually emigrating to Britain to escape Nazism, he questioned the scientific community's understanding of empirical knowledge, asking, "Is it really objective [e.g., disembodied, dispassionate]?" He writes:

> The manner in which the mathematician works his way towards discovery, by shifting his confidence from intuition to computation and back again from computation to intuition, while never releasing his hold on either of the two, represents in miniature the whole range of operations by which articulation disciplines and expands the reasoning powers of man. . . . The alternation between the intuitive and the formal depends on tacit affirmations, both at the beginning and at the end of each chain of formal reasoning.[38]

In elucidating the process of discovery, Polanyi observed that in spite of modernity's hope to achieve rational, objective knowledge, scientific discovery can never be purely cognitive or objective. Even the most objective of scientific knowledge needs embodied intuition, a tacit embodied knowledge that cannot always be rationally articulated, to discover it.[39] Within the scientific community, discovery is grounded in intuition; it is also grounded in an apprentice-style practice of technical skills, methods, and best practices that have been passed down by an authoritative community of scientists. In the scientific community, knowledge is not as rational and objective as one might think; it is embodied, relational, and dependent on others. Polanyi is quick to add that this does not make knowledge subjective but instead clarifies that "comprehension is neither an arbitrary act nor a passive experience, but a responsible act claiming universal validity" that has been developed within a community context that continually tests its connection to reality.[40]

In Polanyi's understanding of tacit, embodied knowledge, the concept of truth also expands. In a Cartesian context, truth is individual, propositional, and entirely rational. In an embodied context, however, the concept of "true" is more like that which Dru Johnson unpacks in his *Knowledge by Ritual*, where he observes that *emeth* (אֱמֶת, commonly translated as "true") in the Old Testament is not used in reference to propositional statements. Drawing on Yoram Hasony's work, Johnson instead notes that *emeth* "captures the fidelity between what is and what ought to be."[41] Carpentry captures this sense of "true," where calling a cut "true" indicates that it fits seamlessly into the project at hand. Something that is *emeth* is sure, real, reliable, and stable;[42] it fits. In the Old Testament context, *emeth* was tested over time, fit within the ultimate reality of God's will, and was lived out in the everydayness of life in community.[43] When embodiment is fundamentally assumed, what is "true" is not simply rational and individual; it is embodied and relational, and as Stanley Hauerwas notes, it is tested as it is lived in community.[44]

Polanyi's description of the process of gaining knowledge in a scientific setting mirrors the process of growing in discernment toward wisdom. Knowledge is not gained in a vacuum separate from the reality of our embodiment and the context, culture, and community in which our embodiment rests. The process of discovery needs the discerning skills of a trusted community to be gained through intuition, trial and error, and guidance from those who have gone before us. Johnson asserts that this process of discernment is the biblical ideal for knowing.[45] Our epistemology is deeply enriched, then, when we view knowledge through our identities as embodied beings, not disembodied minds.

Implications

What might an identity of embodiment mean for the formation of Christian identity? Shifting our deeply embedded understanding of our identities from a "brain on a stick" to an "embodied being" will take more than mind-centered insight (and more than reading this chapter, if it proves convincing). We need to practice the skills of embodied knowing by expanding the notion of Christian disciplines beyond those that Western individualism so highly values. In so doing, we can perhaps expand our understanding of identities as embodied. We may also find ourselves cultivating skills for a more discerning Christian life—one that might aid in some of the angst-filled questions about knowing and doing the right thing that plague so many of my students and perhaps many in the church.

We have seen that an intellect-valuing mind-set casts knowing as an individual pursuit, with mastery of propositional knowledge as the *telos* in our Christian formation. My students are concerned about knowing the correct answer and doing the right things—after all, they have been trained to "ace that test" and "nail that paper." The ability to prove rational knowledge gained through education is a good. We have also seen, however, that an embodiment-valuing mind-set casts knowledge in a different kind of metaphor—one of growth, process, and discovery within the context of an authoritative community that has a body of tradition and knowledge, practices and language, and wisdom of those who have gone before. An embodiment-valuing mind-set views the development of discernment and wisdom as the *telos* in our Christian life, and Christian formation shifts from gaining rational knowledge to the cultivation of skills that helps us develop discernment and wisdom.

Sam Wells likens Christians who undertake the development of discernment to actors who practice improvisation. Good improv does not develop overnight; the actors regularly engage in games to practice skills (such as saying "Yes, and," rather than blocking ideas and scenarios, which also helps their partners look good). Practicing skills develops habits, and cultivating habits develops intuitive responses so that improv actors become skilled at instinctively navigating the unexpected in any given performance. In much the same manner, Christian disciplines hone skills of the Christian life, practicing these skills develops habits, and cultivating habits develops our intuitive responses (our character). Thus, when decisions or life challenges come, we have developed the ability to intuit or discern a way forward, instinctively living out the values of God's kingdom within God's larger story.[46]

The typical North American evangelical context values the practice of individual quiet times for scriptural study and prayer; each Sunday, we emphasize the preaching of the Word. These pursuits are deeply valuable, as they foster skills such as listening to God and discerning propositional truth. What if we trained our congregations to also thoughtfully exercise embodied Christian practices to cultivate a character that instinctively demonstrates the values of God's kingdom? For example, practicing Sabbath, a weekly "time-out" for rest and communal worship, reminds me of my finitude, as I pause and become aware of my body's tiredness from the week, and that my value does not lie in what I achieve. While I might know this cognitively, practicing Sabbath regularly deepens this truth into wisdom. Kneeling with others, in reverence or confession, trains us in humility before God. Raising our hands in worship trains us in adoration. Opening our hands in prayer trains us to receive unconditionally from God. Taking Communion trains us to taste the Lord's goodness and, when taken with others, trains us to see past social status or barriers. The Lord's Supper is a great equalizer—for all are in need.

We know cognitively that God is worthy, gracious, and generous, but exercising embodied practices of worship helps us develop skills toward the virtues of God's kingdom such as humility, adoration, and gratitude, as well as orient our lives around God's grand story. When it comes to making a decision about what job to take, what person to marry, or how to navigate the most recent societal questions, we have been trained to live outside of our own personal interests and to enter into God's story so that our choices fall within God's value system. This process, of course, is slow, messy, and imperfect in this life; Polanyi might say the same of scientific discovery. In this paradigm, questions about God's will, particularly when God seems silent or God's direction is unclear, become less about knowing the right thing to do in our shifting lives and cultural contexts and more about discerning the carpentry-true, reliable way forward in God's larger story.

Whether due to unexamined assumptions that harbor strict Cartesian dualism or a misreading of the ways Paul uses σῶμα and σάρξ in his epistles, North American evangelical culture has tended to neglect the value of our embodiment in discussions of Christian formation. We tend to ignore the body in favor of the "spiritual" or intellectual and seek to conquer it in our efforts to live godly lives. Regardless of metaphysical differences, however, nonreductive physical monists and Thomistic dualists agree: a functional unity of human personhood suggests that we give deeper thought to our identities as embodied beings. Paul's use of σῶμα and scholarship from various disciplines tell us that a primary function of our embodiment is relationality. Broadening our epistemology from a mind-centered rationality to an embodied knowing then lends itself to a deeper understanding of knowing as more than merely propositional. Knowing instead becomes the development of discernment and wisdom. Discernment is a skill that takes embodied practice; its development happens over time as we engage in embodied practices within a Christ-centered community. When these embodied practices aim at developing skills that lead to Christian virtues, we gain the character, even instinct, to know how to engage when facing life decisions, cultural realities, or unexpected circumstances. Our questions become less about knowing the right thing to do and more about the truest way to live.

NOTES

[1] In 1637, Renee Descartes's famous dictum *je pense, donc je suis* ("I think, therefore I am") changed the course of the Western understanding of knowledge. The proposition sometimes known as *the cogito* casts knowledge as an intellectual, rational, mind-based pursuit, and establishes a radical mind-body substance dualism.

[2] Joel B. Green, *Body, Soul, and Human Life: The Nature of Humanity in the Bible* (Grand Rapids, MI: Baker Academic, 2008); Joel B. Green and Stuart L. Palmer, eds., *In Search of the Soul: Four Views of the Mind-Body Problem* (Downers Grove, IL: InterVarsity Press, 2005); Nancey Murphy, *Bodies and Souls, or Spirited Bodies?* (Cambridge: Cambridge University Press, 2006).

[3] Nancey C. Murphy, "Do Humans Have Souls?: Perspectives from Philosophy, Science, and Religion," *Interpretation* 67, no. 1 (2013): https://doi.org/10.1177 /0020964312463192.

[4] Christian Smith, an emergent dualist, lists thirty capacities of the human body (particularly the human brain as it engages with the external world) that allow for human personhood, such as consciousness, volition, remembering, emotion, understanding of another human mind, creativity, and the ability to create meaning. Christian Smith, *What Is a Person?: Rethinking Humanity, Social Life, and the Moral Good from the Person Up* (Chicago: University of Chicago Press, 2011), 27, 42–89.

[5] William Hasker, *The Emergent Self* (Ithaca, NY: Cornell University Press, 2001), 260.

[6] J. P. Moreland, personal interview with Lisa Igram at Talbot School of Theology, La Mirada, CA, March 6, 2017.

[7] J. P. Moreland and Scott B. Rae, *Body and Soul: Human Nature and the Crisis in Ethics* (Downers Grove, IL: InterVarsity Press, 2000), 202.

[8] For an excellent review of the diversity of Greek and Roman philosophic thought on human anthropology, see Craig S. Keener, *The Mind of the Spirit: Paul's Approach to Transformed Thinking* (Grand Rapids, MI: Baker Academic, 2016), 267–78.

[9] Green et al., *Body, Soul, and Human Life*; Murphy, *Bodies and Souls*.

[10] James D. G. Dunn, *The Theology of Paul the Apostle* (Grand Rapids, MI: Eerdmans, 2006), 54.

[11] *Nephesh* is defined by the word cluster of soul, living being, life, self, person, desire, passion, appetite, and emotion. James Strong, *New Strong's Exhaustive Concordance* (Nashville: Thomas Nelson, 2003), sec. 5315.

[12] *Basar* has been translated as anyone, bodies, body, flesh, fatter, gaunt, lustful, man, mankind, meat, men, and person. Strong, *New Strong's Exhaustive Concordance*, sec. 1320.

[13] Mary Timothy Prokes, *Toward a Theology of the Body* (Grand Rapids, MI: Eerdmans, 1996), 58.

[14] For a review of the range and complexity of anthropological thought at the time, see "Appendix A: The Soul in Ancient Mediterranean Thought" in Keener, *The Mind of the Spirit*, 267–78.

[15] For example, Keener describes how Greek and Roman philosophers would have heard Paul's exhortation in Colossians 3:1–2, "Since you've been raised with Christ, devote yourselves to matters above . . . . Let the focus of your thinking be heavenly matters, not earthly ones." He assumes Paul's missional and pastoral goals in

accommodating to culture, saying "Paul's language adapts familiar philosophic idiom for contemplating divine, heavenly reality, but with a specifically Christocentric focus." Keener, *The Mind of the Spirit*, 238.

[16] Keener, *The Mind of the Spirit*, 77.

[17] John W. Cooper, *Body, Soul, and Life Everlasting: Biblical Anthropology and the Monism-Dualism Debate* (Grand Rapids, MI: Eerdmans, 2000), 10.

[18] Prokes, *Toward a Theology*, 15.

[19] Smith, *You Are What You Love*, 3.

[20] J. P. Moreland, interview.

[21] John A. T. Robinson, *The Body* (London: Hymns Ancient and Modern, 2012), 31.

[22] Translated variously as: think, have an attitude of, adopt view(s), concern(ed), intent on, purpose, live in harmony, mind, observes, set their/your minds. Strong, *New Strong's Exhaustive Concordance*, sec. 5426.

[23] Keener, *The Mind of the Spirit*.

[24] Robinson, *The Body*, 29. Note that Gundry views Robinson's understanding of σῶμα as "personality" as an overstatement, saying that Paul specifically uses σῶμα in reference to the physical body. Gundry does, however, see that Paul "personalizes σῶμα as a necessary part of the human constitution and authentic existence." See Robert H. Gundry, *Soma in Biblical Theology: With Emphasis on Pauline Anthropology* (Grand Rapids, MI: Zondervan, 1988), 244.

[25] Rudolf Bultmann and Robert Morgan, *Theology of the New Testament*, trans. Kendrick Grobel (Waco: Baylor University Press, 2007), 227.

[26] Klaus Berger, *Identity and Experience in the New Testament* (Minneapolis: Fortress Press, 2003), 60; Hans Dieter Betz, "The Concept of the 'Inner Human Being' (ὁ ἔσω ἄνθρωπος) in the Anthropology of Paul," *New Testament Studies* 46, no. 3 (2000): 315–41, https://www.cambridge.org/core/journals/new-testament-studies/article/div-classtitlethe
-concept-of-the-inner-human-being-in-the-anthropology-of-pauldiv/B0C3152DD79F0E
429E708ED812277CED.

[27] Dunn, *The Theology of Paul*, 53, 56.

[28] Bruce J. Malina, *The New Testament World: Insights from Cultural Anthropology* (Louisville: Westminster John Knox Press, 2001), 61–62.

[29] Maurice Merleau-Ponty, *Phenomenology of Perception* (London: Forgotten Books, 2015), 148.

[30] Caroline Walker Bynum, *The Resurrection of the Body in Western Christianity, 200–1336* (New York: Columbia University Press, 1995), 11.

[31] Luke Timothy Johnson, *The Revelatory Body: Theology as Inductive Art* (Grand Rapids, MI: Eerdmans, 2015), 79–80.

[32] Daniel J. Siegel, *The Developing Mind: How Relationships and the Brain Interact to Shape Who We Are*, 2nd ed. (New York: Guilford Press, 2015), 21.

[33] Warren S. Brown and Brad D. Strawn, *The Physical Nature of Christian Life: Neuroscience, Psychology, and the Church* (Cambridge: Cambridge University Press, 2012), 56–57. See also Andi Thacker's Chapter Eight for her discussion of attachment theory and neuroplasticity.

[34] Margaret Wilson, "Six Views of Embodied Cognition," *Psychonomic Bulletin and Review* 9, no. 4 (2002): 625–36, https://doi.org/10.3758/bf03196322.

[35] George Lakoff and Mark Johnson, *Philosophy in the Flesh: The Embodied Mind and Its Challenge to Western Thought* (New York: Basic Books, 1999).

[36] Meredith B. McGuire, "Religion and the Body: Rematerializing the Human Body in the Social Sciences of Religion," *Journal for the Scientific Study of Religion* 29, no. 3 (1990): 285.

[37] Esther Lightcap Meek, *Loving to Know: Covenant Epistemology* (Eugene, OR: Wipf & Stock, 2011), 24.

[38] Michael Polanyi, *Personal Knowledge: Towards a Post-Critical Philosophy* (Chicago: University of Chicago Press, 1974), 131.

[39] Polanyi is known in part for his description of tacit knowledge—knowledge that we know but have difficulty articulating, because it is a kind of knowledge that differs from propositional statement. For example, I know how to balance on a bicycle, but if I try to teach a child how to do the same, my words and descriptions will not help much—she needs to experience and practice it until she comes to know for herself what it means to balance on a bicycle. In his words, "We know more than we can tell." Michael Polanyi and Amartya Sen, *The Tacit Dimension* (Chicago: University of Chicago Press, 2009), 4.

[40] Polanyi, *Personal Knowledge*, vii–viii.

[41] Dru Johnson, *Knowledge by Ritual: Biblical Prolegomenon to Sacramental Theology* (Winona Lake, IN: Eisenbrauns, 2016), 75.

[42] Strong, *New Strong's Exhaustive Concordance*, sec. 571.

[43] Johnson, *Knowledge by Ritual*, 76.

[44] Stanley Hauerwas, *Truthfulness and Tragedy: Further Investigations in Christian Ethics* (Notre Dame: University of Notre Dame Press, 1989), 9.

[45] Johnson, *Knowledge by Ritual*, 77.

[46] Samuel Wells, *Improvisation: The Drama of Christian Ethics* (Grand Rapids, MI: Brazos Press, 2004).

Identity of Attachment
How God Shapes Our Neurobiology

ANDI THACKER

L ike many helping professionals, I was drawn to the field of counseling because of my own emotional and relational wounds. Substance abuse, mental illness, and divorce are just a few examples of the negative experiences that have permeated my family story and dramatically impacted my growth, stability, and identity. I have witnessed firsthand the devastation of major mental illness and the destructive path of alcohol dependence. As has been my experience working with other families, as well as my personal experience, the ultimate casualty in these circumstances are the very relationships that form the family.

My pursuit of psychological studies was in part to answer this question: "Is emotional and relational healing even possible for one born into such a family of dysfunction?" My journey has culminated in an understanding of how God embeds people in relationships where heartbreaking wounding does occur, yet these relationships are the very context in which God does the finest work of relational restoration.

In the beginning, God created human beings within the context of relationships for the purpose of interconnection. Because of God's innately relational design, humans are inextricably tied to each other. In the field of psychology, the main caregiver-child relationships that shape and inform one's future relationships are termed one's *attachments*.[1] For the purposes of this work, one's identity is defined as an ongoing process that is based on one's self perceptions and the perceptions and declarations of others.[2] Although identity is multifaceted and impacted by the many contexts in which an individual resides, this chapter will focus on identity as it is influenced by one's main attachment relationships. The way one experiences these early integral relationships as well as later relationships influences how one identifies the self. Further, one's attachment relationships influence one's relationship with God and, in turn, one's identity.

The purpose of this chapter is to integrate attachment research, identity formation, and neural functioning, viewed through the lens of theology. This chapter will explore God's intended attachment design for humans, examine how one's attachment to God influences identity on both an individual and a community level, and investigate how God utilizes relational experiences to bring healing through both vertical and horizontal connections.

Human Development: Created for Connection

From the beginning of the biblical narrative, the human blueprint shows that men and women are created for relationships. In Genesis, prior to the entrance of sin into the world, the narrative highlights both the relational nature of the Godhead as well as the relational nature of humanity: "Then God said, 'Let us make human beings in our image, to be like us' . . . So God created human beings in his own image. In the image of God he created them; male and female he created them" (Gen. 1:26–27 NASB). This verse describes the relational nature of the connection between God the Father, God the Son, and God the Holy Spirit, and highlights how God's intended purpose was to create humans to be image bearers who, like God, are innately relational.[3] Prior to the fall in Genesis 3, Adam and Eve enjoyed untainted relational connectedness with each other and with their Creator. This early picture of interconnectedness illuminates the nature of humanity and human relationships. First, God's intended purpose was to create humans as relational in nature, like the Godhead.[4] Second, because relational interconnectedness existed prior to sin entering the world, the innate human need to be in relationship with God and with others is not a consequence of sin. Third, God intends for humans to experience the joy that results from both a vertical relationship with God and horizontal relationships with others.

Even though human relationships existed prior to the fall, the entrance of sin marred these relationships from Adam and Eve forward. God's original design created humanity for life-giving relationships, and it is within a fractured relational context that wounding occurs as a result of sin. However, God chose the same vehicle, relationships, to bring about healing by allowing Jesus Christ to atone for human sin.[5]

The Relational Foundation

At birth, humans are born into a relational context that lays the foundation from which an individual will operate:

> Attachment research points to the importance of the parent-child relationship in shaping children's interactions with other children, their sense of security about exploring the world, their resilience to stress, their ability to balance their emotions, their capacity to have a coherent story that makes sense of their lives, and their ability to create meaningful interpersonal relationships in the future.[6]

The primary relational context in which an infant seeks support and protection is one's main attachment.[7] This main attachment relationship is set apart from all other relationships and serves as a "home base" from which the infant may venture out and explore his or her world while returning periodically for comfort, satisfaction, and joy. As indicated by psychiatrist and author Curt Thompson, different attachment types represent various ways that a child, and eventually an adult will approach and interact with the world based on previous patterns of interaction with his or her primary caregiver.[8] When attachment occurs optimally, the special relationship between an infant and his or her caregiver is characterized by the infant feeling "seen, safe, soothed, and secure."[9] The foundation of attachment is laid by verbal and nonverbal interactions that occur between the caregiver and infant. In fact, a vast majority of the communication that forms attachment between the infant and caregiver occurs through nonverbal communication.[10] This nonverbal communication, which is characterized by tone of voice, facial expression, bodily movement, and positive touch, communicates far more than words to the developing infant. Main caregivers who create an atmosphere for secure attachment are well attuned to their infant's emotional state and respond appropriately to him or her.[11]

Insecure Attachment

Between Eden and the new heaven on earth, human relationships do not remain untouched by the consequences of sin. The impact of sin on relationships can be seen when optimal attachment experiences do not occur and a child is left with what is known as an insecure attachment. Research indicates that while there is only one form of secure attachment, there are three different types of insecure attachment. Just as a home environment in which the main caregiver is highly attuned to the child's emotional landscape creates a secure attachment, a home in which the main caregiver is not attuned to the child and does not provide such an atmosphere will likely lead to an insecure attachment.[12]

Parents are often unaware of their own attachment histories and how their parenting techniques are impacted by their past experiences. The different types of insecure attachment can be characterized by specific parenting patterns. Thompson notes, "The driving force behind this form of attachment is the manner in which the caregivers respond to their children's emotional states, often without the adults even being aware of the effect of their parenting."[13] The momentary emotional interactions that occur between the main caregiver and child form the building blocks of one's attachment, either secure or insecure.

Avoidant insecure attachment. The first type of insecure attachment is called *avoidant attachment*. A child who grows up in an environment with an avoidant attachment experiences the parent as emotionally distant. The main caregiver in this situation is generally not aware of and does not trust his or her emotions. Because of this distrust, the parent may not express his or her emotions, and may even reject the child's expressed emotions. Avoidant attachment can lead to a child who, like the caregiver, is not very emotionally attuned.[14] These individuals tend to rely on logical, linear processing rather than on emotional input.[15] Avoidant attachment style often results in what is termed *dismissive insecure attachment* in adulthood.[16] Adults who function within this category of insecure attachment tend to be emotionally distant or closed in relationships.

Ambivalent/anxious insecure attachment. The second type of insecure attachment is the ambivalent/anxious attachment style. This style is characterized by a main caregiver who is emotionally intrusive with the child while also behaving inconsistently and unpredictably.[17] Because the child is unable to predict the parent's responses, he or she will experience anxiety and may begin to monitor the parent's emotional state. In adulthood, the ambivalent/anxious attachment style can lead to an adult with a preoccupied attachment style.[18] Adults with preoccupied attachment styles tend to be flooded and overwhelmed by their own emotional states and therefore are unable to adequately attune to the emotional states of others. Because their early attachment experiences lead to the belief that others are unpredictable and unreliable, individuals in this category struggle to trust others.

Disorganized insecure attachment. The final form of insecure attachment is called *disorganized attachment*. This type results from early attachment experiences in which the main attachment figure may abuse the child or create an atmosphere of extreme emotional deprivation that leaves the child in fear of the main caregiver.[19] At times, main caregivers may be diagnosed with significant disorders like bipolar disorder, schizophrenia, or substance dependence disorders. While parents in this category often report a high degree of love for their children, their own difficulties significantly hinder their ability to adequately monitor their child's emotional state and provide consistent and appropriate care. As a result of this type of attachment experience, the child can suffer trauma that leaves him or her frightened and confused, without a sense of safety. Adults with this type of disorganized insecure attachment may live with unresolved trauma.[20]

Attachment Passed Down

Because individuals tend to parent out of their own experiences, attachment styles tend to be perpetuated from generation to generation.[21] An insecure attachment style, however, can be transformed into what is termed *earned secure attachment*. Earned secure attachment occurs when an individual undergoes reparative emotional experiences within the context of relationship. Additionally, research indicates that the single greatest factor impacting the process of earned secure attachment is how well the individual makes sense of his or her own attachment experience.[22]

Because an infant may interact with multiple significant caregivers, it is quite possible that he or she will develop a mixture of attachment styles. The human brain operates as an "anticipation machine" that interprets stimuli through the lens of previous experience; different individuals, therefore, will elicit different responses based on their previous relationships.[23]

The Relational Brain

At birth, the human brain contains about one hundred billion brain cells. During the third trimester of gestation, a developing fetus will begin to have experiences in utero that will cause brain cells to begin to communicate with other brain cells. As the child develops through pregnancy until birth, brain cells will continue to communicate with other brain cells and form connections. All the connections that form within the brain are based on a child's experiences. The firing patterns of brain cells follow what is known as Hebb's axiom, through which "what fires together, wires together."[24] Every time a pattern of brain cells fires or communicates in a pattern, the likelihood increases that those brain cells will fire again in that same pattern. Continued communication along the same pattern will eventually create ruts or pairings within the brain.

In the case of attachment, certain types of relational experiences within the main attachment relationship will create certain pairings within the brain of the child. For example, if a caregiver repeatedly soothes an infant when it cries in distress, the infant's brain will eventually pair soothing and comfort with the presence of the caregiver. Over time, the infant's brain will pair the caregiver with a sense of comfort and will be able to think of or visualize the caregiver when distressed to cause the same firing pattern and create a sense of comfort. With continued activation of the same neuronal communication pattern, the caregiver does not even need to be present for the infant's brain cells to communicate with one another and activate the same communication pattern as if the caregiver were present. As one can imagine, in the caregiver-infant dyad, there are many opportunities for the caregiver to communicate to the infant the elements of secure attachment to create many connections in the brain for secure attachment.[25] The infant with a secure attachment comes to expect similar positive experiences from future relationships.[26] The same is true for insecure attachment styles. As a child's interactions with a main caregiver continue in a similar pattern that is characterized by the different insecure attachment types, the neurobiology of the child will be shaped to reflect those attachment patterns and relational expectations.

Identity Development in the Life-Span

Since a young child does not yet have a developed sense of differentiation between his- or herself and their caregiver, the child will see self through the lens of the caregiver.[27] As a child progresses developmentally, however, he or she will begin to develop differentiation and identify self as separate from the main caregiver(s). Even through the process of differentiation, however, one will continue to identify based on self-perceptions and on others' perceptions and declarations that occur within the main attachment relationship(s).

As indicated by developmental theorist Erik Erikson, the task of identity formation continues and is a prominent developmental experience in adolescence. The core task at this developmental stage is for individuals to explore identity as it relates to one's interests, relationships, and gifts.[28] Although the role of main attachment figures is different during adolescence, the influence of these relationships on identity formation remains highly impactful.[29] Research indicates that as one progresses from adolescence into emerging adulthood, identity formation is very important to the process of engaging in intimate adult relationships.[30] Further, secure intimate relationships serve as a means by which one can find support

149

when one's identity is threatened or in reconsidering previous identity conceptualizations.[31]

Whereas some perceptions that shape one's identity are vocalized, many of the perceptions of others are often communicated nonverbally. Nonverbal communication can be misinterpreted but still be integrated into one's identity. These misinterpretations sometimes come through insecure attachment experiences in which the child might interpret a main caregiver's emotional distance or emotional preoccupation with self as indicative of the child's value or status as an individual. In reality, the main caregiver's interactions with the child very rarely are based on the child but rather are highly influenced by the past neurological wiring of the main caregiver. It is common, however, for children to personalize their experiences with main caregivers in a way that makes sense to them, even though the conceptualization made by the child might not be consistent with the intention of the caregiver.

These differing attachment styles, based on relational experiences with main caregivers, influence how one identifies the self. A child with a secure attachment more easily internalizes an identity of being loved and cherished while accepting the concept that the self and others are trustworthy. For the individual with an avoidant insecure attachment, identity would be more likely characterized by a more logical and linear self-conceptualization. Individuals in this category are often viewed as strong, put together, and distant, perhaps not needing others. This perception of strength and emotional detachment can be integrated into one's identity and impact how one relates to others. For the individual with an ambivalent/anxious attachment style, identity might be characterized by a feeling of anxiety because of the past experience of finding main caregivers to be unreliable. Also, because an individual with an ambivalent/anxious attachment type might be overwhelmed with his or her emotions, this person can be perceived by others as self-absorbed. Individuals within this type are reportedly fearful and jealous in romantic relationships.[32]

Finally, the individual with a disorganized attachment style tends to fear intimacy in relationships and struggles to regulate his or her emotions.[33] This struggle can lead to an internalized identity as one who is unlovable or damaged. Further, individuals who present this attachment style might be perceived by others as difficult in relationships because of their emotional instability and fear of intimacy. Because great variability exists within God's human creation, these themes will not apply to everyone, but these examples demonstrate how one's identity is linked to attachment style.

Attachment and God

Attachment styles not only extend into adulthood and impact later relationships; they also impact one's relationship with God. Thompson has posited that an individual's attachment style is directly related to how one experiences a relationship with God the Father. Christ followers are often unaware of how deeply their childhood relationships impact the trajectory of their relationship with God. An adult who experiences secure attachment in childhood is more likely to trust God as Father. If one's attachment from childhood is insecure, however, this individual will experience similar relational patterns in one's expectation of God the Father. For those who have experienced the avoidant attachment style, God is perceived as distant and cold. God is not seen as a source of comfort or as an emotional being. Rather, God is the prescriber of rules and regulations. For the individual with an ambivalent/anxious attachment, God is conceptualized as unreliable and unpredictable, and even displeased with the individual.[34] For the individual with a disorganized attachment, God is experienced as angry and highly displeased because the earthly attachment experience has been characterized by trauma. It is very common that insecure attachment experiences yield a relationship with God that is characterized by distance and an inability to feel an emotional connection with God.

A. W. Tozer, in his work *Knowledge of the Holy*, states that "what comes into our minds when we think about God is the most important thing about us."[35] While what comes to mind when we think about God is highly influenced by our knowledge of God, I propose that what we think about God is influenced more by our attachment style(s), as well as our identity. Thompson has asserted that attachment style is highly influential over one's relationship with God.[36] I would take this a step further to include that both one's attachment style and one's identity highly influence a person's capacity for intimacy with God the Father. Depth of knowledge and impeccable theological understanding about the Godhead can have little impact on one's ability to be in relationship with God.

By the same token, one's identity and attachment style will influence how one intersects with the body of Christ. Because early attachments lay the foundation from which an individual will operate relationally, early patterns of relatedness will follow an individual into adulthood. The body of Christ is not devoid of relational difficulties and disagreements, and many of these challenges originate in how one operates relationally based on previous attachment experiences. Further, how one conceptualizes one's identity as part of the body of Christ will be informed by how one conceptualizes relationships. For individuals who experience secure attachment as a child, interacting with the body of Christ may be easier, because their expectation for relationships is that they will be safe or have the possibility for safety. The individual who has experienced insecure attachment, however, may regard others in the body of Christ with suspicion or distrust. The relational expectations that spring forth from early insecure attachment hinder the way God intends for the body of Christ to function. Rather than a place for vulnerability and healing, the body of Christ becomes a context for suspicion and distrust. These feelings can be further compounded when individuals within the body of Christ have wounding experiences that confirm their suspicions and deepen their distrust in others. While these wounding experiences do happen, the identity and expectations of an individual with insecure attachment also shape how they experience certain events; they often react very differently than someone with a secure attachment experience. Fortunately, relationships characterized by wounding are not the end of the story. God utilizes relationships to bring restoration, even when similar relationships have been the vehicle for brokenness.

Relational Rupture

Because the impact of sin extends to all human relationships, every relationship is characterized by relational ruptures. Some ruptures are healthy and warranted for the safety of a relationship; these are called *limit-setting ruptures*. A second form of rupture is called a *benign rupture*. Benign ruptures are "minor separations in . . . relationships that can be repaired without too much effort."[37] Benign ruptures are often based on misunderstandings or unintentional mishaps within relationships. In children, benign ruptures can provide an opportunity to expand the window of distress tolerance for a child when a parent is well-attuned to the child and can quickly and relatively easily repair the rupture. These opportunities help children grow into adults who have the emotional capacity to regulate their own emotions, as well as tolerate distress in interpersonal relationships. The third form of relational rupture, which is the most destructive, is the toxic rupture. Toxic ruptures occur when an individual experiences mental and emotional pain that is overwhelming and deeply painful as a result of interpersonal interactions.[38] Sin births toxic ruptures, even if the consequence of the rupture is not immediately experienced. Even though toxic ruptures carry cataclysmic consequences for all involved, the acts that lead to them can sometimes seem minor. However, even wounding that appears to be minor can cut deeply to the core of an individual's well-being.

All ruptures influence one's identity, and toxic ruptures, which are often based in shame, can lead an individual to believe certain messages that are not consistent with what Scripture says about an individual. For instance, an individual who has a repeated experience in which individual worth is evaluated based on outward appearance, ability, or worldly success will likely form the belief that "I am only valuable relationally when I am at my best." This belief, of which the individual is often not aware, will strongly influence identity and relational attachments. The result is a belief system that is generally not consistent with an individual's theological understanding but rather is consistent with one's operational theology in how one chooses to live day-to-day.

Relational Repair

Relationship ruptures are a frequent aspect of living between Eden and God's new creation; this life thus is not about eliminating ruptures but rather about repairing ruptures when they do occur.[39] When sin entered the world in Genesis 3, Adam and Eve caused a rupture between themselves and God. God, however, created a pathway to heal ruptures, and this pathway to restoration is formed from relationship. All healing occurs

153

within the context of that relationship, and a person's spiritual healing occurs because of Jesus Christ's atoning death on the cross.[40] In addition to healing one's relationship with God through Christ, God utilizes human relationships to bring healing to wounded souls. As God intricately heals the wounds of brokenness through reparative relational experiences, an individual can begin to integrate and transform his or her identity to one that is based on earned secure attachment.

Earned Secure Attachment

Even though one's attachment style typically endures from childhood into adulthood, an insecure attachment style can be transformed into an earned secure attachment style. Earned secure attachment occurs when one experiences relationships that are characterized by empathic caring. Since the brain continues to make neural connections throughout one's life, the brain of an individual with an insecure attachment from childhood will anticipate having similar relational experiences as before. When a person experiences a different kind of relationship, however, the brain has the opportunity to form different neural connections or pairings.[41] Over time, if an individual experiences relationships that are characterized by empathic understanding, his or her brain will form new connections that can result in earned secure attachment. Because the human brain is complex and nonlinear, small and seemingly insignificant changes can create huge neurological rewards.[42] These small experiences of empathy can create substantial neurological changes that lay the foundation for earned secure attachment. James K. A. Smith has expanded upon this point, proposing that Christian discipleship is more about addressing one's habits rather than increasing one's knowledge.[43] Therefore, simply increasing one's knowledge of God will not be transformative of one's relationship with God. One must experience habitual transformation within the context of relationship to influence change in one's relationship with God and others.

While the relational changes that lead to earned secure attachment often occur within horizontal relationships, one's vertical relationship with God can also lead to earned secure attachment. Thompson has pioneered a guided imagery technique that can be utilized to facilitate a sense of secure attachment within one's relationship with God.[44] The exercise aims to create new neural pathways for thinking about God that are based on the truth of Scripture, rather than dictated by the wounds of previous insecure attachments. Because of the tendency to view God through the lens of previous attachment experiences, one must rewire one's brain to truly understand and experience a perfect God. Thompson's imagery exercise guides an individual through a process of mentally imaging and experiencing God as God "speaks" the truth of Scripture over the individual. The words one needs to image to heal attachment wounds are contrary to the messages one received as a child. With repeated use, one can begin to cultivate a reparative attachment experience with God. This guided imagery exercise is only one of many examples of how one's attachment story can be transformed.

Since much of what comprises one's identity of attachment is based on messages received through relationships, as one's attachment experiences begin to change, one's identity will also change. One's beliefs about one's self can no longer be based on negative relational experiences, but rather on reparative relational experiences. This leads an individual to conceptualize identity more consistently with what Scripture says about who one is and self-understanding.

Concluding Thoughts

One's identity of attachment is formed within the context of early interpersonal relationships and lays the relational foundation for the remainder of one's life. Through these early attachments, one develops an identity that is based on both positive and negative relational experiences. Through God's original design and intent, relationships serve as a vehicle for healing both with God and others. Through authentic relationships, one can experience true relational healing that is transformative to one's attachment and identity on a neurological, emotional, and spiritual level.

I am a witness both professionally and personally of how God can bring healing to families through the very relationships that were so destructive. God has healed relationships in my life that I thought were impossibly marred by dysfunction. However, through God's extraordinary kindness and mercy, these relationships have been restored. At each family gathering, I am reminded that what evil meant for harm, God has used to bring redemption and restoration (Gen. 50:20). This is the amazing message we share as Christians: no matter what one's life experiences, hope remains. The hope that God offers—to reshape one's neurobiology and identity—is by the same mechanism, relationship, that first created the wound. God is making all things new (Rev. 21:5).

NOTES

[1] Allan Schore and Judith Schore, *The Science of the Art of Psychotherapy* (New York: W. W. Norton, 2012), 27.

[2] Jenny McGill, *Religious Identity and Cultural Negotiation: Toward a Theology of Christian Identity in Migration* (Eugene, OR: Pickwick, 2016), 16–17.

[3] Robert A. Pyne, "Created in the Image of God," in *Understanding Christian Theology*, ed. Charles R. Swindoll and Roy B. Zuck (Nashville: Thomas Nelson, 2003), 674–75.

[4] Pyne, "Created in the Image of God," 674–75.

[5] Millard J. Erickson, *Christian Theology*, 2nd ed. (Grand Rapids, MI: Baker Books, 1998), 830.

[6] Daniel J. Siegel and Mary Hartzell, *Parenting from the Inside Out: How a Deeper Self Understanding Can Help You Raise Children Who Thrive* (New York: Penguin Group, 2003), 101–2.

[7] Mario Mikulincer and Phillip R. Shaver, *Attachment in Adulthood: Structure, Dynamics, and Change*, 2nd ed. (New York: Guilford Press, 2016), 15.

[8] Curt Thompson, *Anatomy of the Soul: Surprising Connections between Neuroscience and Spiritual Practices That Can Transform Your Life and Relationships* (Carol Stream, IL: Tyndale House Publishers, 2010), 119.

[9] Daniel J. Siegel, *Brainstorm: The Power and Purpose of the Teenage Brain* (New York: Bantam Books, 2013), 145.

[10] Schore and Schore, *Science*, 28.

[11] Siegel and Hartzell, *Parenting*, 103. Although a child's main caregiver is oftentimes the child's parent, sometimes main caregivers are other significant people in a child's life. For the purposes of this discussion, the terms *caregiver* and *parent* will be used interchangeably.

[12] Siegel, *Brainstorm*, 145–49.

[13] Thompson, *Anatomy of the Soul*, 122.

[14] Curt Thompson, *Soul of Shame: Retelling the Stories We Believe about Ourselves* (Downers Grove, IL: InterVarsity Press, 2015), 53.

[15] Thompson, *Anatomy of the Soul*, 123.

[16] Daniel J. Siegel, *Mindsight: The New Science of Personal Transformation* (New York: Bantam Books, 2011), 174.

[17] Thompson, *Anatomy of the Soul*, 127.

[18] Siegel, *Mindsight*, 174.

[19] Thompson, *Anatomy of the Soul*, 130–31.

[20] Siegel, *Mindsight*, 174.

[21] Daniel Hill, *Affect Regulation Theory: A Clinical Model* (New York: W. W. Norton, 2015), 96.

[22] Siegel and Hartzell, *Parenting*, 125, 34.

[23] Hill, *Affect Regulation Theory*, 91.

[24] Bonnie Badenoch, *Being a Brain-Wise Therapist: A Practical Guide to Interpersonal Neurobiology* (New York: W. W. Norton, 2008), 7, 9.

[25] Siegel, *Brainstorm*, 145.

[26] Thompson, *Soul of Shame*, 43.

[27] John W. Santrock, *Lifespan Development*, 15th ed. (New York: McGraw Hill Education, 2015), 177.

[28] Santrock, *Lifespan Development*, 372.

[29] Kaylin Ratner, "The Role of Parenting and Attachment in Identity Style Development," *The University of Central Florida Undergraduate Research Journal* 7, no. 1 (2017): 15–26, https://www.urj.ucf.edu/docs/ratner.pdf.

[30] Joe F. Pittman et al., "Attachment, Identity, and Intimacy: Parallels between Bowlby's and Erikson's Paradigms," *Journal of Family Theory and Review* 3, no. 1 (2011): 32–46, http://doi.org/10.1111/j.1756-2589.2010.00079.x.

. [31] Pittman et al., "Attachment, Identity, and Intimacy," 40.

[32] Santrock, *Lifespan Development*, 435.

[33] Thompson, *Anatomy of the Soul*, 130.

[34] Thompson, 118, 123, 127.

[35] A. W. Tozer, *Knowledge of the Holy: The Attributes of God* (San Francisco: HarperOne, 2009), 1.

[36] Thompson, *Anatomy of the Soul*, 117.

[37] Thompson, 189.

[38] Thompson, 188–90.

[39] Thompson, *Soul of Shame*, 53.

[40] Robert A. Pyne, *Humanity and Sin: The Creation, Fall, and Redemption of Humanity* (Nashville: Thomas Nelson, 1999), 246–47.

[41] Daniel J. Siegel, *The Mindful Brain Reflection and Attunement in the Cultivation of Well-Being* (New York: W. W. Norton, 2007), 129.

[42] Theresa A. Kestly, *The Interpersonal Neurobiology of Play: Brain-Building Interventions for Emotional Well-Being* (New York: W. W. Norton, 2014), 59.

[43] James Smith, K. A., *You Are What You Love: The Spiritual Power of Habit* (Grand Rapids, MI: Brazos Press, 2016), 33.

[44] Thompson, *Anatomy of the Soul*, 143.

Identity as Christian and Gendered

The Case for Particularity

NATE COLLINS

The relationship between gender and identity has been the subject of intense discussion and debate over the past hundred years. From the pioneering anthropologists and sexologists of the early 1900s, to the crests and valleys of the various waves of feminism that have swept the academy, scholars have labored to describe the nature and extent of gender's influence on personal identity. In doing so, they have posed and provided responses to a wide variety of questions, such as: Does an individual's gender tell us anything about his or her personhood? Is it always, for example, linked to biological sex? Does gender ever change, or is it always the same? Across cultures? Across time? In individual people? Is gender necessarily binary, or can there be more than two genders? Do cultural ideas about masculinity and femininity reflect anything intrinsic to gender itself?

In addition to these questions, however, evangelical Christians have their own doctrinal priorities to consider when constructing a theology of the relationship between gender and identity. For example, does the creation narrative in Genesis 1 and 2 communicate anything about the meaning and purpose of gender? Or does the creation narrative assert anything about the relationship between gender and sex difference? Between gender and sexuality? Do souls have gender? What truths does the Bible contain about the relationship between personhood and gender?

The issue raised by this last question points to an even more specific set of questions that are of unique interest to Christians—namely, theological questions about anthropology and the historical plan of salvation that unfolds in the Bible. In other words, if gender was originally created by God, how was this divine intent affected by the fall in Genesis 3? Furthermore, how does the redemption of human personhood affect gender? And finally, what will gender look like in the Eschaton?[1]

Obviously, one chapter cannot adequately address all of these questions. At the same time, the variety of concerns these questions reflect are themselves evidence of the swirling complexities involved in the phenomenon of gender identity. Due to this complexity, the possibility exists that current evangelical modes of doctrinal investigation have not prepared evangelical thinkers to engage these questions. This chapter will, therefore, aim at a particularly circumscribed goal—namely that of reflecting on a few preliminary theological and philosophical perspectives that might support the development of a contemporary doctrine of gender. In particular, an evangelical doctrine of gender that is not adequately coordinated with critical realist epistemology is unnecessarily prone to the attacks of postmodernism. Furthermore, such a doctrine of gender will only withstand the cultural forces of postmodernism and moral relativism if it is grounded in a biblical anthropology. For this reason, this chapter will suggest that a critical realist approach to gender theory can be compatible with a biblical anthropology of personhood in general and Christian identity in particular.

Why Critical Realism?

In order to understand the relevance of critical realism in a Christian attempt to formulate a doctrine of gender, we need to conduct a brief survey of the past 150 years or so of ideas that form the historical and conceptual backdrop for contemporary gender theory. During the second half of the nineteenth century in the Western world, several central themes of the Enlightenment—particularly humanism, individual autonomy, and the right to self-governance—made it possible for women to reflect upon and draw attention to their disadvantaged political position. These themes largely coalesced into women's suffrage movements in individual countries, but they were also harbingers of subsequent feminist groups that attempted to expand women's access to additional social benefits that had generally been limited to men.

A Brief History of Feminism

In general, gender theorists present the history and development of feminism as a slow transition away from essentialist accounts of gender identity toward social constructionist perspectives. Moreover, most gender theorists acknowledge that this transition has unfolded in a series of "waves" of feminist discourse and activism. The first modern gender essentialists were actually early anthropologists in the second half of the nineteenth century who modeled their studies of human gender and sexuality after studies of the animal world. In time, the work of these anthropologists consolidated into a brand-new field of study known today as sexology.[2] The core belief of these essentialists is that gender identity itself is not only encoded in bodily structures, but manifests in culturally transcendent behaviors, norms, and ideals.[3] From this perspective, evaluating authentic "man-ness" and "woman-ness" is an empirical matter that one can measure by holding up individual men and women to the essentialist standard.[4]

Social constructionist accounts of gender, on the other hand, reflect a fundamentally different approach to its meaning. Constructionists believe that gender identity is a cultural artifact that emerges out of the physical structures of the body but is not reducible to or explainable solely on the basis of those structures. In other words, societies base gender identity upon biological sex, but these identities may or may not resemble each other across time and culture. For a social constructionist, authentic "man-ness" in North America might look nothing like authentic "man-ness" in Sub-Saharan Africa, because there is no culturally transcendent way for a male human person to be a man.[5]

Beginning with the publication of Simone de Beauvoir's 1949 pioneering work, *The Second Sex*, this basic distinction between sex (a biological term) and gender (a sociocultural term) has fueled the development of contemporary fields of feminism and contemporary gender theory.[6] While the first wave of feminist activism subsided once women gained the right to vote in most Western countries, a second wave emerged as feminist theorists focused their efforts on a much more nebulous task: identifying specific cultural structures and forces that had shaped and influenced the construction of feminine identities in the West so that they could, in turn, be reshaped in more just ways.[7]

One of the central problems that emerged early in the development of feminist theory centered on the concept of Otherness. The importance of this term became evident as early as the work of de Beauvoir in *The Second Sex*, in which she states:

> Humanity is male and man defines woman not in herself but as relative to him; she is not regarded as an autonomous being. . . . For him she is sex—absolute sex, no less. She is defined and differentiated with reference to man and not he with reference to her; she is the incidental, the inessential as opposed to the essential. He is the Subject, he is the Absolute—she is the Other.[8]

This use of the term "Other" points to a second major theme within second wave feminism that began to develop alongside the theme of equality: the idea that "difference" itself often derives its significance from socially constructed standards and norms. In other words, feminists began to emphasize the reality that men are not simply different from women in the way that apples are different from oranges, but in societies characterized by gender inequality they are also different from women in the way that white and black people were in South Africa during apartheid.

Decades of efforts to illuminate the social processes through which feminine identities had become sites of Otherness resulted in a wide variety of approaches to understanding the relationship between gender, inequality, and difference.[9] Over time, many gender theorists determined that the burgeoning number of these approaches actually constituted a third wave of feminism, despite its diversity of approaches to the subject matter of gender and women's liberation. The lack of a unifying theme notwithstanding, the various approaches to feminism and gender theory in third wave feminism in general can be framed as either a product of or a reaction against the project of identity politics.[10]

Feminism and Particularity

Feminism and identity politics are frequently associated with each other today, but in reality their relationship is much more complicated. In philosophical terms, the tension stems from the different approaches that third wave feminists and gender theorists take in relating identity and particularity.[11] While second wave feminism regarded feminine identity as sufficiently monolithic to warrant a "big-tent" approach to addressing gender inequalities, third wave gender theorists are much more circumspect in their generalizations about "women's experience" or "women's oppression." For example, many black women did not feel that white feminist scholars understood their unique experience enough to represent their interests.

This reluctance—and in some cases outright refusal—to conduct the feminist enterprise beneath the unified banner of "Woman" reflects a renewed appreciation of the reality that feminism itself is not immune to the socializing influence of culture. To paraphrase Alasdair MacIntyre, gender theorists began asking questions such as "Whose femininity? Which particularity?"[12] Not only do gender theorists respond to these questions differently among themselves, but some believe that the questions are actually unanswerable. These disagreements are rooted in fundamentally different approaches to resolving the problem that particularity poses to the project of identity.[13]

Critical Realism and a Christian Doctrine of Gender Identity

Despite the current proliferation of perspectives within third wave feminism, it seems possible for a fresh understanding of gender and identity to emerge that takes the problem of particularity seriously. Such an endeavor would need a philosophical underpinning that is able to stabilize the concept of gender identity (as distinguished from biological sex) without producing a framework that collapses under the weight of a naïve essentialism. In short, I believe that critical realism offers just that.

I will limit my discussion of critical realism here to a brief interaction with an important edited volume entitled *Reclaiming Identity: Realist Theory and the Predicament of Postmodernism*.[14] This specific work is particularly helpful because it explicitly addresses the interconnection between personal identity and realist theory, which is fairly close to what I am exploring in this chapter. After a brief explanation in the introduction of both the postmodern critique of essentialism and the resulting dethronement of objective knowledge in philosophical discussions about identity, coeditor Paula M. L. Moya claims:

> Prevailing theories of identity lack the intellectual resources to distinguish between different kinds of identities. We contend that a theory of identity is inadequate unless it allows a social theorist to analyze the epistemic status and political salience of any given identity and provides her with the resources to ascertain and evaluate the possibilities and limits of different identities. Neither "essentialist" nor "postmodernist" theories of identity can do this.[15]

Moya suggests that this endeavor to illuminate the "epistemic status and political salience of . . . identity" is possible because the postmodernist critique of the possibility of objective knowledge is based on an overly restrictive definition of what counts as "objective." According to Moya, postmodernism understands objective knowledge as "knowledge that is completely free of theoretically mediated bias," while a postpositivist perspective like critical realism happily acknowledges that "(1) all observation and knowledge are theory mediated and that (2) a theory-mediated objective knowledge is both possible and desirable."[16] In other words, truth claims can be both fallible and defensible because they are also revisable.[17]

A second benefit of critical realism, according to Moya, is the manner in which it embraces the reality that knowledge is enmeshed with social practices, which enables theorists to "recognize the causal constraints placed by the social and natural world on what humans can know."[18] This results in a tendency to deemphasize the distinction between facts and values that was popular in positivist accounts of knowledge:

> [B]ecause humans' biologically and temporally limited bodies enable and constrain what we are able to think, feel, and believe and because our bodies are themselves subject to the (more or less regular) laws of the natural and social world, realists know that what humans are able to think of as "good" is intimately related to (although not monocausally determined by) the social and natural "facts" of the world. Consequently, realists contend, humans' subjective and evaluative judgments are neither fundamentally "arbitrary" nor merely "conventional." Rather, they are based on structures of belief that can be justified (or not) with reference to their own and others' well-being. These judgments and beliefs, thus, have the potential to contribute to objective knowledge about the world.[19]

This second characteristic of a critical realist approach to identity will be particularly useful in our discussion of theological anthropology. In short, it sheds light on the fecundity of personal experience as a source of salient identity claims.

Furthermore, despite the relative brevity of this introduction to critical realism, its relevance to feminist questions about identity is hopefully self-evident. Indeed, the presence of a viable alternative to both essentialist and social constructionist accounts of gender identity suggests that perhaps the problems of particularity are overblown. Whether or not secular feminism is able to overcome them, however, is not my primary concern. For this reason, it is now time to look at specific resources within the Christian tradition that should inform a theological anthropology of gender. This endeavor could unfold in a variety of ways, so the following discussion will focus on elements within a Christian anthropology that dovetail nicely with the preceding discussions about feminism and critical realism.

Perspectives from Theological Anthropology

Human personhood can be viewed through three lenses: creation, relationality, and history. First, human personhood exists in an embodied state in both the first creation and the new creation. In the first creation account in Genesis 1, the author emphasizes the sexuate character of personhood by explicitly stating that humanity was created "male and female" (Gen. 1:27).[20] Since the embodiment of human personhood is rooted in the doctrine of creation, it is reasonable to believe that it was designed to unfold according to a particular paradigm—namely that which was intended by the One who created it. In other words, human embodiment has an end and purpose, but this end must be achieved according to a particular pattern. Not just any paradigm for manifesting one's embodiment will do.

Another aspect of the embodiment of human personhood is that it is encapsulated by physical borders, or boundaries. These boundaries tell me where "I" ends and "not-I" begins, which means that they also play a role in characterizing individual human personhood. In other words, individual people are more than their bodies, but human personhood is at least embodied personhood.

Viewing personhood through the second lens, relationality, showcases the social character of human personhood. Although it is commonplace today—to the point of cliché—to assert the intrinsic relationality of personhood, it is nonetheless important to reflect on the implications of this assertion for other theological loci within Christian doctrine, especially gender. In fact, the second creation story in Genesis 2 confirms the intrinsic relationality of humankind, because the author frames the creation of woman throughout the chapter as a resolution to a unique dilemma: the incompleteness of humankind.

Unfortunately, English translations of Genesis 2:18 obscure this dilemma by the way they translate the Hebrew word אָדָם ('adām, humankind, man, Adam) in the statement "It is not good for the man to be alone . . ."[21] The standard word for *man* is an entirely different word, אִישׁ ('īsh), and it only appears at the end of the narrative of Genesis 2 in verse 23 when Adam states, "She shall be called 'woman,' for she was taken out of man." In other words, the word 'īsh is an intrinsically gendered term in ways that the word 'adām simply is not.[22] A better translation, perhaps, of the statement of the problem in Genesis 2:18 might be something like "It is not good for humankind to be solitary." In other words, the creation of the woman was a solution to an anthropological problem of cosmic proportions and not simply a solution to the presumed loneliness of Adam.[23]

Two additional details confirm this elevated role of woman in connection to the relationality of humankind. First, the text of Genesis refers to the woman using the Hebrew term עֵזֶר (*'ēzer*) in verses 18 and 20, a term rendered in virtually every major translation as "helper." This choice is problematic, however, because elsewhere in the Hebrew Scriptures the word is almost universally translated as "savior" or "rescuer." In other words, it refers to a superior party who comes to the aid of one in dire need, not simply to an assistant who exists to make one's life easier. A second detail in verse 24 confirms this: the man clings to the woman, his rescuer, not the reverse.

When viewed through the lens of history, the developmental character of personhood becomes most apparent. Personal stories of growth, change, and development are unveiled by the steady, plodding process of history. In one sense, a historical approach to personhood mediates between the embodied nature of personhood and the relationality of personhood. Once individuals are born into this world, they are embodied with a bend toward relationship. The individual persons they become, however, can only be discovered through the passage of time. As history unfolds, personhood itself emerges and develops within its surrounding matrix of relationships and events.

In a well-known passage from his book *Allegory of Love*, C. S. Lewis addresses a common misunderstanding about the so-called "stages" we go through as our personhood develops and matures. According to Lewis, "humanity does not pass through phases as a train passes through stations: being alive, it has the privilege of always moving yet never leaving anything behind. Whatever we have been, in some sort we are still."[24] Although Lewis's words likely refer to humanity as a whole, the same is true with regard to individual people.

Theological Anthropology of Gender

When these three anthropological perspectives—personhood as created, relational, and historical—are combined together, they yield at least three distinct implications for a Christian doctrine of gender identity. In this final section, I will describe these implications and explore how they might be related to Christian identity in particular.

Constrained, but Not Determined

The first of these implications is that while gender identity is constrained by embodiment, it is not wholly determined by it.[25] This implication results from viewing the embodiment of personhood through the lens of relationality and history. The embodiment of personhood shapes gender identity in unavoidable ways that are nonetheless not wholly determinative in themselves.

In order to grasp how this implication relates to gender identity, one must remember the distinction between biological sexuate difference and gender difference. From the perspective of theological discourse, God created biological sex as a transcendent binary, and gender as an immanent binary.[26] A transcendent binary is one that exists across time and culture, while an immanent binary exists only in specific, concrete situations. In other words, a woman can be described as a female person anatomically for the same reasons across time and culture, while the elements that form her gender identity—that is, the shape of both her self-understanding as feminine and her public identity as a woman—are tied to her particular culture.[27]

At the same time, a Christian understanding of salvation history acknowledges that the created intent behind both sex and gender is not always perfectly realized in a post-fall world. The fall impairs the proper functioning of human bodies, so that the physical and social constraints experienced in and because of these bodies are sometimes amplified in ways that can frustrate human flourishing. In other words, human bodies are physical structures that are inherently constraining, but post-fall, they can also become sites of dysfunction.

One extreme example of these constraints is the approximately sixteen varieties of intersex conditions that geneticists have identified. According to the medical community, an intersex condition is any physical, hormonal, or genetic anomaly that renders an individual's sex ambiguous. For example, individuals with Turner syndrome appear to be female, but they lack a second X chromosome (e.g., their karyotype is 45,XO) and are usually infertile.[28] Another condition known as Klinefelter syndrome affects males who inherit an extra X chromosome from either their father or mother (e.g., their karyotype is 47,XXY). Nongenetic intersex conditions include females with clitoromegaly (an enlarged clitoris) or males with a micropenis and undescended testes, as well as conditions such as androgen insensitivity syndrome in genetic males and congenital adrenal hyperplasia in genetic females. Gender identity is constrained in each of these cases in unique ways by the embodiment of personhood and in ways that are not entirely determinative.[29]

Porous, but Not Unbounded

A second doctrinal implication is that gender identity is porous but not unbounded. Like the previous implication, this aspect of gender surfaces when we view the relational aspect of personhood through the lens of embodiment and development. Understanding the human person in this way is especially important today because it represents a course correction in response to the widespread modern error of viewing people as isolated individuals. For many, however, the permeability of personhood might seem to be an overcorrection to understanding personhood as embodied or as encapsulated by boundaries. After all, what good are boundaries if they are constantly in flux and always susceptible to external forces?

Philosopher Charles Taylor notes this dilemma and suggests that the emphasis on individualism is a relatively recent development in Western culture. The concept of solitary personhood stands in opposition to the way premodern cultures thought about personhood.[30] Commenting on Taylor's analysis, James K. A. Smith explains that "the premodern self's porosity means the self is essentially *vulnerable* . . . . To be human is to be essentially *open* to an outside (whether benevolent or malevolent), open to blessing or curse, possession or grace."[31] In essence, Taylor reminds us of the implications of recovering a premodern understanding of the self; if personhood is impermeable, then the external world, including other persons (human or divine), is powerless to exert any influence on it. If personhood, however, is porous, then who we are is susceptible to outside influence by the external world, including other persons. This means that our personhood changes as a result of our interpersonal connections, and we become different persons.

When applied to gender, this concept of porous or permeable personhood suggests that the content of an individual's gender identity can change in response to his or her external world, including social interactions with others. This potential for change also highlights the importance of distinguishing between transcendent sex identity and immanent gender identity. In some social contexts, changes in the content of an individual's gender identity are minimal. When a group of friends who gather every Monday night to play poker begin teasing one of the men for his music preferences, that individual might not necessarily think of himself as a different kind of man from the others. In situations like these, it is clear that stereotypes are at work that ultimately fail to adequately reflect reality. In other words, social responses to this kind of particularity are often not meaningful enough to challenge the overall content of an individual's gender identity.

Social responses to other kinds of particularity, however, suggest that some phenomena have an acculturated, gendered meaning associated that is significant. In the United States, for example, while entertaining a fondness for Taylor Swift may not require a man to turn in his "man card," he had better not be caught wearing eyeliner, for example. Wearing makeup is an example of one particularity whose cultural significance contains a gendered component, because wearing makeup is predominantly associated with being a woman.

Some extreme forms of particularity have so much cultural significance attached to them that they can serve as the basis for grouping individuals together who exhibit that form of particularity into one social category. In situations like this, labels will often emerge that index a stand-alone identity of sorts that contains a gendered component. I refer to these kinds of social identities as "secondary gender identities" because their function is to specify what kind of man or woman someone is on the basis of this or that form of particularity.

Sexual orientation, for example, is a form of particularity that is sufficiently meaningful in contemporary Western culture to be the basis for group identities to form around labels like "gay" and "lesbian."[32] In some circumstances, it might be meaningful or important for an individual to clarify that he or she is not straight but is, in fact, a gay man or a lesbian woman. In other words, "man" and "woman" are the two primary gender identities that refer to straight and nonstraight people alike, while "gay" and "lesbian" function as secondary gender identities that further specify the sexual orientation of the individual.

Contingent, but Not Arbitrary

A third and final doctrinal implication of the embodied, relational, and developmental character of personhood is that gender emerges from contingent, but not arbitrary, sociohistorical processes. Much like the previous two implications, this aspect of gender results from viewing the developmental character of personhood through the lens of embodiment and relationality. The content of one's gender identity—that is, the way that one identifies as a man or a woman, not merely as a male person or a female person—is in part a function of one's social context, which means that when it changes, it changes for a reason. More specifically, it responds to specific social phenomena within history.

There was a time in human history, for example, when sexual orientation was insufficient as a type of particularity to function as the basis of a gendered social category. As the disciplines of sexology and psychology developed, however, the social landscape began to change. First, scholars in these fields began to theorize about the phenomenon of orientation itself, instead of merely on sexual behavior of either a heterosexual or homosexual kind. Second, individuals who were not heterosexual began to reflect publicly on how their orientation affected their day-to-day lives. And third, a public consensus concerning orientation began to develop that regarded heterosexuality as a gendered standard that one had to meet, rather than as one form of particularity among others. Although cultural attitudes in North America have begun to shift, until the twenty-first century, part of becoming a man was proving that one was not gay.

The development of the gay identity as a secondary gender identity within contemporary Western culture is evidence of the sociohistorically contingent, but not arbitrary, character of gender identity. It emerged in response to a specific set of social conditions that are difficult to predict and impossible to reverse.[33] At the same time, the current form of the gay identity is not the same as the form it took in the 1970s, and it will likely not be identical to the way that nonstraight people twenty years from now will understand the relationship between their orientation and their primary gender identity. As a developmental feature of gender identity, the modern gay identity might adapt to subsequent features of human culture in ways that are less tied to gender and sexuality. It is nonetheless important to note that this adaptation is not simply "going back to the way things were," because, like cultural artifacts, identities change, carrying bits of their history with them.

Concluding Remarks about Gender and Christian Identity

Christians who want to think deeply about how their Christian identity relates to their gender identity can only align with God's intended design if they rightly prioritize the questions that need to be answered. Age-old questions about "biblical gender roles," as well as questions about contemporary phenomena like transgender identities are important, but our answers to them will be impoverished to the extent that we neglect deeper matters related to the ontology of gender and God's intent behind it.

In this chapter, I have attempted to make the case that Christians who subscribe to a form of critical realism are striving for better, more accurate ways to describe reality, including gender. What I have attempted to accomplish here is to outline some helpful components that can both form and inform a more in-depth exploration of what gender is, how it is enculturated, and how it develops. When gender identity emerges, it does so in the context of a physical body that constrains its final shape without fully determining it. The generative nature of human culture, coupled with the spiritual effects of the fall, both influence the way that gender identity is embodied. Furthermore, the permeability of personhood suggests that gender identity itself is porous, even as it maintains distinct boundaries. Gender cannot simply mean whatever we want it to mean, but sometimes it means more than we know. And finally, the historical character of personhood suggests that gender identity also develops contingently in relationship to real social phenomena and not, therefore, in an arbitrary fashion. Realists are concerned with what actually exists, not that which could have been otherwise.

What might this mean for the way that concrete gender identities are related to Christian identity? I have argued elsewhere that the second creation account links masculinity with the concepts of order and structure and femininity with the concepts of fullness and relationship.[34] But instead of viewing these concepts as traits or roles to embody, I suggest we view them as principles that give individual gender identities meaning. In other words, the feminine principle of relationship can be a source of gendered meaning for women no matter their cultural background, or even their individual character traits for that matter.

If this is the case, then relating one's spiritual identity as a Christian to one's gender identity becomes a matter of stewarding the principles of masculinity or femininity in the context of one's own embodiment of gender. A man can steward the masculine principle of order whether his personality of personal strengths are stereotypically masculine or not. Similarly, a woman with stereotypically masculine personality traits can still resonate with her gender identity as a woman if she views it through the lens of her spiritual identity as a Christian—that is, as an opportunity to steward the feminine principle of relationship.

Although the task of constructing a Christian doctrine of gender is far from complete, it can now utilize the parallel benefits between a critical realist approach to identity and a Christian understanding of personhood. Indeed, the existence of such fruitful connections bodes well for future theological development of a Christian understanding of what God intended in creating, from the beginning, "male and female."

NOTES

[1] At the intersection of questions about gender difference and salvation history are even more questions that are clustered around the idea that the Bible characterizes masculinity and femininity in terms of an intrinsic hierarchy of authority. These are actually hybrid questions, however, because they depend on assumptions about the nature of gender itself, as well as an understanding of how gender differences are affected by the events in salvation history. Virtually everyone agrees that the Bible contains traces of patriarchy, but disagreement abounds regarding the source of this patriarchy. Complementarians believe that hierarchal gender roles are part of the original created order, while egalitarians believe that they are a product of the fall. Plenty of ink has already been spilled in this particular debate, so my discussion here will address other important and perhaps more fundamental theological dilemmas that have been neglected in contemporary evangelical scholarship on the subject of gender.

[2] See, for example, Havelock Ellis, *Studies in the Psychology of Sex* (New York: Random House, 1942). See also William H. Masters and Virginia E. Johnson, *Human Sexual Response* (Toronto: Bantam Books, 1966) and *Human Sexual Inadequacy* (Toronto: Bantam Books, 1970).

[3] Note that essentialism is not the same as complementarianism. The belief that gender identity is ground in culturally transcendent essences is separate from the belief that gender identity is manifest in differentiated roles in church leadership and marriage that are characterized by a functional hierarchy.

[4] Determining what, exactly, is the approved standard is the central problem that gender essentialists try to solve. For a popular example of gender essentialism, see John Gray, *Men Are from Mars, Women Are from Venus* (New York: HarperCollins, 1992).

[5] For an extended discussion about how feminists use the epistemology of social constructionism in their theory and activism, see Sally Haslanger, "Social Construction: The 'Debunking' Project," in *Socializing Metaphysics: The Nature of Social Reality*, ed. Frederick F. Schmitt (Lanham, MD: Rowman and Littlefield, 2003).

[6] For the sake of historical accuracy, it is important to note that Simone de Beauvoir was first and foremost a committed Marxist who believed that economic inequality was the cause of women's inequality. She never actually embraced the term "feminist" until much later in her career, when she came to realize that women's liberation was a cause that required its own stand-alone effort.

[7] Most feminists classify liberal feminism, socialist feminism, and radical feminism—collectively known as the Big Three—as the primary characters in second wave feminism. For an accessible introduction to the Big Three, as well as subsequent developments in feminist theory, see Chris Beasley, *What Is Feminism? An Introduction to Feminist Theory* (London: Sage Publications, 1999). For an in-depth exploration of the entire modern feminist enterprise, see Susan Archer Mann, *Doing Feminist Theory: From Modernity to Postmodernity* (New York: Oxford University Press, 2012).

[8] Simone de Beauvoir, *The Second Sex*, trans. H. M. Parshley (New York: Bantam Books, 1952), xvi. Examine the effects of this "Othering" of woman in Betty Friedan, *The Feminine Mystique* (New York: W. W. Norton, 1963).

[9] For example, an entire group of approaches often collectively referred to as "French feminism" emerged in the 1980s and continues to influence contemporary feminist theory. Scholars associated with French feminism include Luce Irigaray, Hélène Cixous, and Julia Kristeva.

[10] For the role that identity politics has played in the development of feminist theory, see James Joseph Dean, "Thinking Intersectionality: Sexualities and the Politics of Multiple Identities," in *Theorizing Intersectionality and Sexuality*, ed. Yvette Taylor, Sally Hines, and Mark E. Casey (New York: Palgrave Macmillan, 2011), 121–27.

[11] Although feminist theorists usually use the term "difference" to refer to the wide array of personal experiences that are in some way identity-constituting, I prefer the more descriptive term "particularity."

[12] Alasdair MacIntyre, *Whose Justice? Which Rationality?* (Notre Dame: University of Notre Dame Press, 1989).

[13] Some responses are simply more balkanized forms of feminism, such as the lesbian feminism of Monique Wittig. According to Wittig, lesbians are not women because the identity "woman" is constructed by a heterosexual system of meaning. See Monique Wittig, *The Straight Mind and Other Essays* (Boston: Beacon, 1992), 21–32. Intersectional and standpoint feminists, however, demonstrate a more chastened method of grappling with the problem of particularity, specifically the unique experiences of women of color in the United States. Black legal scholar Kimberlé Crenshaw coined the term "intersectionality" in order to draw attention to the compounded injustice that individuals experience when they are the victims of intersecting axes of discrimination. See Kimberlé Crenshaw, "Demarginalizing the Intersection of Race and Sex: Feminist Critique of Antidiscrimination and Antiracist Politics," *The University of Chicago Legal Forum 1* (1989): 139–67. Other important women of color who are scholars in the broad field of feminism include Patricia Hill Collins, bell hooks, Alice Walker, and Clenora Hudson-Weems. Finally, the poststructuralist feminism of Judith Butler and other queer theorists represents an entirely different kind of solution to the problem of particularity. Butler claims that the endless sets of differences among women render the category of gender meaningless outside specific social contexts, in Judith Butler, *Gender Trouble: Feminism and the Subversion of Identity* (New York: Routledge, 1990).

[14] Paula M. L. Moya and Michael R. Hames-Garcia, *Reclaiming Identity: Realist Theory and the Predicament of Postmodernism* (Berkeley: University of California Press, 2000).

[15] Linda Martín Alcoff, "Who's Afraid of Identity Politics?," in *Reclaiming Identity: Realist Theory and the Predicament of Postmodernism*, ed. Paula M. L. Moya and Michael R. Hames-Garcia (Berkeley: University of California Press, 2000), 7.

[16] Alcoff, "Who's Afraid of Identity Politics?"

[17] For an introduction to the connection between critical realism and a Christian epistemology that incorporates the category of divine revelation, see David K. Clark, *To Know and Love God: Method for Theology* (Wheaton, IL: Crossway, 2003). For an in-depth examination of the philosophical and hermeneutical issues involved, see Kevin J. Vanhoozer, *The Drama of Doctrine: A Canonical Linguistic Approach to Christian Doctrine* (Louisville: Westminster John Knox, 2005).

[18] Alcoff, "Who's Afraid of Identity Politics?," 14.

[19] Alcoff, 14.

[20] I refer to the sexed difference between male and female using the term "sexuate," instead of the much more common term "sexual," because the latter is too closely associated in the English language with the actual act of intercourse.

[21] See the NASB: "Then the LORD God said, 'It is not good for the man to be alone; I will make him a helper suitable for him.'" ESV: "Then the LORD God said, 'It is not good that the man should be alone; I will make him a helper fit for him.'" NIV: "The LORD God said, 'It is not good for the man to be alone. I will make a helper suitable for him.'"

[22] For a discussion of the three technical uses of the word *'adām* in the creation account (a shorthand reference to humankind in general, a reference to the man as a stand-in for humanity in general, and as a proper name), see Richard D. Hess, *Splitting the Adam: The Usage of* Ādām *in Genesis I–V* (Leiden: Brill, 1990), 1–15. See also my discussion of Genesis 1 and 2 in Nate Collins, *All but Invisible: Exploring Identity Questions at the Intersection of Faith, Gender, and Sexuality* (Grand Rapids, MI: Zondervan, 2017), 203–15.

[23] Evidence from the text of Genesis 2 indicating that Adam experienced anything resembling loneliness is lacking. Perhaps he was lonely, or perhaps he just wanted to know what else God intended to create to solve the problem of the heretofore solitary character of humanity.

[24] C. S. Lewis, *Allegory of Love: In Medieval Tradition* (Oxford: Oxford University Press, 1977), 1.

[25] See the nuanced discussion on the relationship between gender and the sexed body in Miroslav Volf, *Exclusion and Embrace: A Theological Exploration of Identity, Otherness, and Reconciliation* (Nashville: Abingdon, 1996), 184–87.

[26] The secular discourse of biology, however, would point to the existence of intersex persons as evidence that sexuate difference is not intrinsically binary, and the secular discourse of human anthropology would point to societies with so-called third genders as evidence that gender identity is not intrinsically binary. For a thorough introduction to the concept of "third sex/gender," see Gilbert H. Herdt, *Third Sex, Third Gender: Beyond Sexual Dimorphism in Culture and History* (New York: Zone Books, 2003).

[27] For a helpful discussion about the interrelationship between public identity and self-understanding, see Alcoff, "Who's Afraid of Identity Politics?"

[28] A male karyotype is 46,XY (e.g., a total of 46 chromosomes, including an X and a Y chromosome) and a female karyotype is 46,XX (e.g., a total of 46 chromosomes, including two X chromosomes).

[29] This is not to say that intersex men and women are incapable of incorporating a coherent gender identity into their self-understanding. At the same time, intersex individuals can only do so by stretching the categories of "man" and "woman," because their gender identity is necessarily less grounded in physical structures.

[30] See discussion in Charles Taylor, *Sources of the Self: The Making of the Modern Identity* (Cambridge, MA: Harvard University Press, 1989), 35–36.

[31] Original emphasis. James K. A. Smith, *How (Not) to Be Secular: Reading Charles Taylor* (Grand Rapids, MI: Eerdmans, 2014), 29.

[32] For an exploration of this connection between sexual orientation and gender, see Collins, *All but Invisible*, 243–69.

[33] Historians approach the task of exploring the development of gay identity in a variety of ways. Traditionally, these attempts have been archaeological in nature, as

gender theorists looked for signs of homosexuality in ancient sources. This was the approach of John Boswell, *Christianity, Social Tolerance, and Homosexuality: Gay People in Western Europe from the Beginning of the Christian Era to the Fourteenth Century* (Chicago: University of Chicago Press, 1980). David Halperin adopts an alternative, genealogical approach that explores the historical conditions that made present realities possible, if not inevitable. See David M. Halperin, *One Hundred Years of Homosexuality: And Other Essays on Greek Love* (New York: Routledge, 1990).

[34]Collins, *All but Invisible*, 209–15.

Epilogue

JENNY MCGILL

B eing human inherently means pursuing an understanding of our-selves. In light of modern events such as white nationalist rallies in Charlottesville, Kenya's election nullification, South Sudan's civil war, North Korea's saber-rattling, the Nashville statement regarding marriage and sexuality, and the dismissal of the Deferred Action for Childhood Arrival (DACA) immigration measure (all of which transpired over the course of four weeks as I concluded the writing of this book), I am struck by the conflicting ways that humanity creates meaning, and by how central, elusive, extensive, and disputed identity-making is. How timely and valu-able this book is to encourage us to evaluate what individual identities we privilege over our central identity in Christ.

In Part One, Chapter One, Jürgen Schulz sets the stage for our discus-sion by grounding identity in the original pristine condition of humanity to its subsequent impiety—one that resulted in a sense of shame and long-ing that still pervades the human experience. In Chapter Two, Rod Reed quickly introduces the remedy for our brokenness through the provision of God in Jesus Christ. Following God's demonstration of love through

Christ, the Christian's primary identity is one who loves, not merely one who believes intellectually. Beliefs that are honestly held lead to action, and Christian spiritual formation must emphasize this holism (John 14:15–31; James 2:14–26). Given our continued existence of frailty, brokenness, and a world of wounding, in Chapter Three Célestin Musekura marks the path for progress: self-identification with the oppressor as we ourselves are oppressors (Matt. 6:12) and paving the way for reconciliation through forgiveness (Matt. 18:22). Can we identify as Christians while continuing to hold others' debts over them when God in Christ no longer holds our debts over us (Matt. 18:23–35)? Indeed, Marc-André Caron takes this discussion further in Chapter Four when he suggests that one's identity in Christ compels him or her not only to forgive others but to identify with other believers as family (2 Cor. 5:14–15). This creates a kinship connection through the blood of Christ (Eph. 1:3), which, once adopted, cannot be extinguished. This is not to say one cannot move between church memberships, but it does mean that one's identity as a Christian depends upon being within a community of faith. More, it connotes a sense of belonging and loyalty to each other that the world longs for (Rom. 12:4–5; Eph. 4:15–16; 1 Cor. 12:25–26) and notices (John 17:18–23). Caron goes on to argue that as Christian identity becomes ostracized, we can take heart in the example of the community in Hebrews: their persecution for their faith was mitigated by their self-identity in being related to each other as siblings of God's family. Christians must neither fear increasing alienation in a pluralistic and secular society nor fight in desperate reaction to it; identification as Christ's community may be best and most authentically forged under pressure, as Jehu Hanciles posits for the Jewish community in exile centuries ago (Jer. 24:4–7; 1 Pet. 1:3–7).[1] Without an adequate self-understanding of one's identity of shame, love, forgiveness, and membership in God's family, one's Christian identity remains stilted and ill-formed.

Part Two departs from an analysis of central themes of identity in the Hebrew and Greek Testaments to begin a discussion of Christian identity within the context of contemporary debates. In view of the furor surrounding refugees, undocumented migration, and wall-building, in Chapter Five, I challenge the reader to consider one's Christian identity as migratory. As migrants, Christians depart from who they thought they were in order to follow Christ and his way of being (e.g., doing), and thus they belong to the family of God in a manner that surpasses even their ties with their biological relatives. Moreover, in their identification with Christ, they are transformed by an identity of displacement—a willingness to be changed to his likeness (2 Cor. 3:18) and to be displaced for the sake of others (Phil. 2:3–8). One's Christian identity remains ineffective so long as self-interest overrides one's identification with the way of the cross (Isa. 53; Matt. 19:20–22; Luke 14:25–27; John 12:24–26; Rev. 3:17–18).

In Chapter Six, Andrew B. Spurgeon argues convincingly that Indian Christians, although they belong to a minority identity, can be both culturally Indian and religiously Christian. The author's passion in fighting for legitimate status in that context helpfully reminds us of the difficulties that minority identity groups face. In Chapter Seven, Lisa Igram makes a stellar case for Christians to embrace their physicality as well as their mentality by asserting that both of these aspects of identity comprise true spirituality. Christian identity integrally involves self-identification as an embodied being. In Chapter Eight, Andi Thacker complements the preceding chapters by elaborating on how God intimately uses our physicality, the actual biological functioning of our neurology, to overcome the relational wounding described in Chapter One. Our human (e.g., relational) identity is remarkably ruptured and repaired through relationships with God and others. We are not fatalistically doomed to the relations into which we were born; our self-understanding and identities are renewed and refashioned by God the Father because of God the Son through the power of God the Spirit, which is manifested in part through the community of faith that Caron mentions in Chapter Four (Isa. 43:18–19; 65:17; Eph. 2:15; 4:24; Rev. 21:5). Nate Collins's closing chapter heralds God's original and intentional creative design for gendered human identity. While the power of sin darkens our interpretation and application of gender, he suggests that understanding human experience through a critical realist perspective will help us pursue the Christian identity God intends for us.

The work of this multiracial and multicultural panel of contributors begs a few last points. As has been elucidated elsewhere,[2] relationality is central to personhood, what it means to be human, and to the performance of Christian identity. These contributors have extended the discussion, such as how Schulz describes the onset of shame, the human condition in Genesis, as principally a broken relationship. Reed and Musekura elaborate on how love and forgiveness are essential to Christian identity in repairing lost relationships. Caron emphasizes how communal solidarity among Christians related to one another as children of God mitigates against the pains of persecution. Igram relays how both mind/spirit and body are embedded fundamentally in relation that the two, working in tandem however detached, hints to humanity's original psychophysical unity, which will be re-wed (Gen. 2:7, 25; 3:7, 22; Eph. 1:9–10; Rev. 21:3–4; 22:3). Igram, Reed, and Thacker particularly point out that knowledge and truth are not merely informational and individual knowing but the relational knowing of embodied creatures.

These individual works demonstrate that while identity-making is central to the human endeavor of meaning-making, identity-making for Christians is chiefly a communal endeavor. Christians are responsible to each other in being responsible to God (Eph. 4:25; 1 Cor. 5:10–12). The mind-set of how we act is a community effort as we live as the body of Christ (1 Cor. 10:16–17; Eph. 4:15–16). As Christians, we must acknowledge our shame, commit to love, pursue forgiveness, embrace solidarity, and allow our self-understanding to be subject to God and one another. The authors in Part Two demonstrate this by describing our identity as Christians as migrant, embodied, relationally attached, and gendered. Our primary belief as Christians is that identity is based on what God has revealed (Eph. 1–2; Rev. 22:6). One of my professors, Glenn Kreider, once remarked, "truth is not relative, but it is perspectival," and we desperately depend upon God's perspective—revealed through creation, God the Son, God the Spirit, the Scripture, and the body of Christ—because our language, interpretations, and intellects fail us (Rom. 1:18–20; 2 Tim. 3:16–17). Christian identity is formed by faith in the "three-who-are-one" God[3] who is faithful to us (2 Tim. 2:13; 1 John 4:9).

Lastly, while rituals, relationships, and restrictions help define one's identities,[4] Christian identity-making must not be forged in fear. It seems many Christians in the United States today struggle against the country's shift from a cultural Christianity to an alienated Christianity. No one wants to lose a position of power, convenience, and ease, but to fight this cultural phenomenon with white-knuckled determination is not the way of Jesus Christ. Jesus gave up everything voluntarily, graciously, willingly. Are we kind, brave, generous, temperate (Phil. 2:14–15), or are we self-protective, defensive, brash, or brazen? Dietrich Bonhoeffer argued that Christians are not to live unscathed lives when he asserted, "The Christian, too, belongs not in the seclusion of a cloister life but in the thick of foes,"[5] and our goal is not to rail against reality but to serve (Mark 10:45). We will suffer loss, but avoiding unfair treatment is not our primary goal. As Caron argues, we should position ourselves to live sacrificially (e.g., paying someone's rent or mortgage this month). Christian identity is not merely about discovering who we are, but about showing ourselves to be the holy temple of God (Eph. 2:19–22). What representations of God do we show to others through our lives?

We see and know only in part (1 Cor. 13:12; 1 John 3:2–3), and only those who are pure in heart will see God (Matt. 5:8). God's purifying love—burn though it may, as it drains our well-stained dross—must purify our hearts (Titus 2:14; 1 John 1:9). May we as Christians understand our position in Christ solidly enough to release our tightly held individualistic inclinations in the pursuit of the common good for the life of the world.[6] Christian identity is a self-conception that starts with a personal understanding of the legitimate shame of dishonor before a holy God, moves into an identity of forgiveness and love based on Christ's example, and ends with a willingness to identify with his suffering (Rom. 8:17; 1 Pet. 4:13). Christian identity, far from self-gratification (although this comes as a by-product), calls us to live a life that is scathed by sacrifice (John 12:24–26). Performing one's Christian identity, in its various cultural forms, is a scandalous and scary calling. We can do better (Rom. 15:13; Gal. 5:22–23).

NOTES

[1] Jehu Hanciles, *Beyond Christendom: Globalization, African Migration, and the Transformation of the West* (Maryknoll, NY: Orbis, 2008), 147.

[2] Stanley J. Grenz, "The Social God and the Relational Self: Toward a Theology of the Imago Dei in the Postmodern Context," in *Personal Identity in Theological Perspective*, ed. Richard Lints, Michael S. Horton, and Mark R. Talbot (Grand Rapids, MI: Eerdmans, 2006); Christian Smith, *What Is a Person?: Rethinking Humanity, Social Life, and the Moral Good from the Person Up* (Chicago: University of Chicago Press, 2011).

[3] This Trinitarian description of God is borrowed from Doug P. Baker, *Covenant and Community: Our Role as the Image of God* (Eugene, OR: Wipf & Stock, 2008).

[4] See Taiye Selasi's TED talk, during which she discusses these. "Don't Ask Me Where I'm from; Ask Where I'm a Local," TED video, filmed October 7, 2014, at TEDGlobal 2014,16:05, https://www.ted.com/talks/taiye_selasi_don_t_ask_where _i_m_from_ask_where_i_m_a_local.

[5] Dietrich Bonhoeffer, *Life Together*, trans. John Walter Doberstein (New York: Harper, 1954), 17.

[6] This phrase is taken from a video produced by the Acton Institute. "For the Life of the World: A Letter to the Exiles—Official Trailer," YouTube video, 3:18, February 13, 2014, https://www.youtube.com/watch?v=7DE-Zk_kLYk.

Bibliography

Alcoff, Linda Martín. "Who's Afraid of Identity Politics?" In *Reclaiming Identity: Realist Theory and the Predicament of Postmodernism*, edited by Paula M. L. Moya and Michael R. Hames-Garcia, 335–41. Berkeley: University of California Press, 2000.

Allen, Diogenes. *Spiritual Theology: The Theology of Yesterday for Spiritual Help Today*. Cambridge, MA: Cowley Publications, 1997.

Alsup, Wendy. "Apologetics for Women." *Fathom*, July 17, 2017. https://www.fathommag.com/stories/apologetics-for-women-1.

Alwin, Duane F., Jacob L. Felson, Edward T. Walker, and Paula A. Tufiş. "Measuring Religious Identities in Surveys." *Public Opinion Quarterly* 70, no. 4 (2006): 530–64.

Ambedkar, B. R. "Who Were the Shudras?" In *Babasaheb Ambedkar: Writings and Speeches*, edited by Vasant Moon. Bombay: Education Department, Government of Maharastra, 1990.

Anderson, Neil T. *The Bondage Breaker*. Eugene, OR: Harvest House Publishers, 1993.

Andrews, Charles R. *Mahatma Gandhi: His Life and Ideas*. Delhi, India: Jaico Publishing House, 2005.

Asumang, Annang, and Bill Domeris. "The Migrant Camp of the People of God: Theme for the Epistle to the Hebrews." *Conspectus* 3, no. 1 (2007): 1–7.

Aune, David E. *The New Testament in Its Literary Environment*. Philadelphia: Westminster, 1985.

Averbeck, Richard E. "The Bible in Spiritual Formation." In *The Kingdom Life: A Practical Theology of Discipleship and Spiritual Formation*, edited by Alan Andrews, 277–304. Colorado Springs: NavPress, 2010.

Avrahami, Yael. "בוש in the Psalms— Shame or Disappointment?" *Journal for the Study of the Old Testament* 34, no. 3 (2010): 295–313.

Baago, Kay. *A History of the National Christian Council of India, 1914–1964.* Nagpur, India: The National Christian Council, 1967.

Backhaus, Knut. "How to Entertain Angels: Ethics in the Epistle to the Hebrews." In *Hebrews: Contemporary Methods—New Insights*, edited by Gabriella Gelardini, 149–75. Boston: Brill, 2005.

Badenoch, Bonnie. *Being a Brain-Wise Therapist: A Practical Guide to Interpersonal Neurobiology.* New York: W. W. Norton, 2008.

Baker, Doug P. *Covenant and Community: Our Role as the Image of God.* Eugene, OR: Wipf & Stock, 2008.

Barth, Karl. *Church Dogmatics.* Vol. 1. Edinburgh: T&T Clark, 1956.

Basu, Moni. "9 Myths about Hinduism—Debunked." *CNN Belief Blog*, April 25, 2014. http://religion.blogs.cnn.com/2014/04/25/9-myths-about -hinduism-debunked/comment-page-1/.

Bauer, Walter. *A Greek-English Lexicon of the New Testament and Other Early Christian Literature (BDAG).* Edited by Frederick W. Danker. Chicago: University of Chicago Press, 2000.

Bauerschmidt, Frederick Christian. "Thomas Aquinas: The Unity of the Virtues and the Journeying Self." In *Unsettling Arguments: A Festschrift on the Occasion of Stanley Hauerwas's 70th Birthday*, edited by Charles R. Pinches, Kelly S. Johnson, and Charles M. Collier, 25–41. Eugene, OR: Cascade, 2010.

Bauks, Michaela. "Neuere Forschungen zum altorientalischen Seelebegriff am Beispiel der Anthropogonien." In *Anthropologie(n) des Alten Testaments*, edited by Jürgen van Oorschot and Andreas Wagner, 91–116. Leipzig: Evangelische Verlagsanstalt, 2015.

Beasley, Chris. *What Is Feminism? An Introduction to Feminist Theory.* London: Sage Publications, 1999.

Bebbington, David W. *The Dominance of Evangelicalism.* Oxford: Oxford University Press, 2005.

Bechtel-Huber, Lyn. "The Biblical Experience of Shame/Shaming: The Social Experience of Shame/Shaming in Biblical Israel in Relation to Its Use as Religious Metaphor." PhD diss., Drew University, 1983.

Berger, Klaus. *Identity and Experience in the New Testament.* Minneapolis: Fortress Press, 2003.

Berger, Peter, L. *A Rumor of Angels: Modern Society and the Rediscovery of the Supernatural.* New York: Doubleday, 1969.

———. *The Sacred Canopy.* New York: Doubleday, 1967.

Berger, Peter L., and Thomas Luckmann. *The Social Construction of Reality: A Treatise in the Sociology of Knowledge.* New York: Doubleday, 1966.

Betz, Hans Dieter. "The Concept of the 'Inner Human Being' (ὁ ἔσω ἄνθροπος) in the Anthropology of Paul." *New Testament Studies* 46, no. 3 (2000): 315–41. Accessed March 26, 2017. https://www.cambridge .org/core/journals/new-testament-studies/article/div-classtitlethe-concept -of-the-inner-human-being-in-the-anthropology-of-pauldiv/B0C3152DD79 F0E429E708ED812277CED.

Bonhoeffer, Dietrich. *Life Together.* Translated by John Walter Doberstein. New York: Harper, 1954.

Borooah, Vani K., Amaresh Dubey, and Sriya Iyer. "The Effectiveness of Jobs Reservation: Caste, Religion and Economic Status in India." *Development and Change* 38, no. 3 (2007): 423–45.

Boswell, John. *Christianity, Social Tolerance, and Homosexuality: Gay People in Western Europe from the Beginning of the Christian Era to the Fourteenth Century.* Chicago: University of Chicago Press, 1980.

Brennan, Katherine Harrison. "No Place for Exile: How Christians Should (Not) Make Sense of Their Place in the World." *Australian Broadcasting Corporation,* December 16, 2016. http://www.abc.net.au/religion/articles/2 016/12/16/4593491.htm.

Brown, Warren S., and Brad D. Strawn. *The Physical Nature of Christian Life: Neuroscience, Psychology, and the Church.* Cambridge: Cambridge University Press, 2012.

Bruce, Alexander B. "The Synoptic Gospels." In *The Expositor's Greek Testament,* edited by W. Robertson Nicoll, 1–651. Grand Rapids, MI: Eerdmans, 1956.

Bubash, Paul. "Dalit Theology and Spiritual Oppression: A Call to Holiness in a Universal Church." *Journal of Theta Alpha Kappa* 38, no. 2 (2014): 36–51.

Bultmann, Rudolf, and Robert Morgan. *Theology of the New Testament.* Translated by Kendrick Grobel. Waco: Baylor University Press, 2007.

Butalia, Urvashi. "Let's Ask How We Contribute to Rape." *The Hindu,* December 25, 2012. http://www.thehindu.com/opinion/op-ed/lets-ask -how-we-contribute-to-rape/article4235902.ece.

Butler, Judith. *Gender Trouble: Feminism and the Subversion of Identity.* New York: Routledge, 1990.

Bynum, Caroline Walker. *The Resurrection of the Body in Western Christianity, 200–1336*. New York: Columbia University Press, 1995.

"Cabinet Approves Amendments in Constitution (Scheduled Castes) Order, 1950." *Sify News*, February 1, 2017. http://www.sify.com/news/cabinet-approves-amendments-in-constitution-scheduled-castes-orders-news-national-rcbnL5fajbeee.html.

Campbell, William S. *Paul and the Creation of Christian Identity*. London: T&T Clark, 2006.

Cavanaugh, William T. "Migrant, Tourist, Pilgrim, Monk: Mobility and Identity in a Global Age." *Theological Studies* 69, no. 2 (2008): 340–56.

Clark, David K. *To Know and Love God: Method for Theology*. Wheaton, IL: Crossway, 2003.

Clines, David J. A. *The Dictionary of Classical Hebrew, Volumes 1–8*. Sheffield: Sheffield Phoenix Press, 2011.

Coe, John. "Resisting the Temptation of Moral Formation, Opening to Spiritual Formation in the Cross and the Spirit." *Journal of Spiritual Formation & Soul Care* 1, no. 1 (2008): 54–78.

Collins, Nate. *All but Invisible: Exploring Identity Questions at the Intersection of Faith, Gender, and Sexuality*. Grand Rapids, MI: Zondervan, 2017.

Cooper, John W. *Body, Soul, and Life Everlasting: Biblical Anthropology and the Monism-Dualism Debate*. Grand Rapids, MI: Eerdmans, 2000.

Crenshaw, Kimberlé. "Demarginalizing the Intersection of Race and Sex: Feminist Critique of Antidiscrimination and Antiracist Politics." *The University of Chicago Legal Forum I* (1989): 139–67.

de Beauvoir, Simone. *The Second Sex*. Translated by H. M. Parshley. New York: Bantam Books, 1952.

de Caussade, Jean-Pierre. *Abandonment to Divine Providence*. Translated by E. J. Strickland. St. Louis: B. Herder, 1921.

Dean, James Joseph. "Thinking Intersectionality: Sexualities and the Politics of Multiple Identities." In *Theorizing Intersectionality and Sexuality*, edited by Yvette Taylor, Sally Hines, and Mark E. Casey, 119–39. New York: Palgrave Macmillan, 2011.

deSilva, David A. *Despising Shame: Honor Discourse and Community Maintenance in the Epistle to the Hebrews*. Rev. ed. Atlanta: Society of Biblical Literature, 2008.

———. *Honor, Patronage, Kinship and Purity: Unlocking New Testament Culture*. Downers Grove, IL: InterVarsity Press, 2010.

Dharamraj, Havilah, and Angukali V. Rotokha. "History, History Books and the Blue Jackal." In *Indian and Christian: Changing Identities in Modern India, Papers from the First Saiacs Annual Consultation*, edited by Cornelis Bennema and Paul Joshua Bhakiaraj, 14–37. Bangalore, India: SAIACS Press, 2011.

Dhruvarajan, Vanaja. *Hindu Women and the Power of Ideology*. Granby, MA: Bergin & Garvey, 1989.

Di Vito, Robert. "Old Testament Anthropology and the Construction of Personal Identity." *The Catholic Biblical Quarterly* 61, no. 2 (1999): 217–38.

Dietrich, Jan. "Human Relationality and Sociality in Ancient Israel: Mapping the Social Anthropology of the Old Testament." In *What Is Human? Theological Encounters with Anthropology*, edited by Eve-Marie Becker, 23–44. Göttingen: Vandenhoeck & Ruprecht, 2017.

Dunn, James D. G. *The Theology of Paul the Apostle*. Grand Rapids, MI: Eerdmans, 2006.

Dyer, Bryan R. "Suffering in the Face of Death: The Social Context of the Epistle to the Hebrews." PhD diss., McMaster Divinity College, 2015.

Elliot, David. "The Christian as Homo Viator: A Resource in Aquinas for Overcoming 'Worldly Sin and Sorrow.'" *Journal of the Society of Christian Ethics* 34, no. 2 (2014): 101–21.

Ellis, Havelock. *Studies in the Psychology of Sex*. New York: Random House, 1942.

Erickson, Millard J. *Christian Theology*. 2nd ed. Grand Rapids, MI: Baker Books, 1998.

Evans, C. Stephen. "Is There a Basis for Loving All People?" *Journal of Psychology and Theology* 34, no. 1 (2001): 78–90.

Friedan, Betty. *The Feminine Mystique*. New York: W. W. Norton, 1963.

Gabrielson, Jeremy. "Paul's Non-Violent Gospel: The Theological Politics of Peace in Paul's Life and Letters." PhD diss., University of St. Andrews, 2011.

Gandhi, Mohandas K. *None High, None Low*. Bombay: Bharatiya Vidya Bhavan, 1975.

Garland, David E. *The NIV Application Commentary*. Grand Rapids, MI: Zondervan, 1998.

George, S. K. *Gandhi's Challenge to Christianity*. Ahmedabad, India: Navajivan Publishing House, 1947.

Gesenius, Wilhelm, Rudolf Meyer, and Herbert Donner. *Hebräisches und Aramäisches Handwörterbuch über das Alte Testament*. Berlin: Springer, 2013.

"Girls in India Marked for Death." *The Christian Century* 112, no. 10 (March 22, 1995): 324.

A Girl's Right to Live: Female Foeticide and Girl Infanticide. Geneva: NGO Committee on the Status of Women, 2007. https://wilpf.org/wp-content/uploads/2014/07/2007_A_Girls_Right_to_Live.pdf.

Global Knowledge Partnership on Migration and Development. *Migration and Remittances: Recent Developments and Outlook*. Washington, DC: The World Bank, April 2016. http://pubdocs.worldbank.org/en/661301460400427908/MigrationandDevelopmentBrief26.pdf.

Goffman, Erving. *The Presentation of Self in Everyday Life*. Garden City, NY: Doubleday, 1959.

Gray, John. *Men Are from Mars, Women Are from Venus*. New York: HarperCollins, 1992.

Green, Joel B. *Body, Soul, and Human Life: The Nature of Humanity in the Bible*. Grand Rapids, MI: Baker Academic, 2008.

Green, Joel B., and Stuart L. Palmer, eds. *In Search of the Soul: Four Views of the Mind-Body Problem*. Downers Grove, IL: InterVarsity Press, 2005.

Grenz, Stanley J. "The Social God and the Relational Self: Toward a Theology of the Imago Dei in the Postmodern Context." In *Personal Identity in Theological Perspective*, edited by Richard Lints, Michael S. Horton, and Mark R. Talbot, 70–94. Grand Rapids, MI: Eerdmans, 2006.

———. *Theology for the Community of God*. Nashville: Broadman & Holman, 1994.

Grohmann, Marianne. "Diskontinutität und Kontinuität in alttestamentlichen Identitätskonzepten." In *Religionsgemeinschaft und Identität: Prozesse jüdischer und christlicher Identitätsbildung im Rahmen der Antike*, edited by Markus Öhler, 17–42. Neukirchen-Vluyn: Neukirchener Theologie, 2013.

Grund, Alexandra. "'Und Sie schämten sich nicht' Zur alttestamentlichen Anthropologie der Scham im Spiegel von Genesis 2–3." In *Was ist der Mensch, dass du seiner gedenkst (Psalm 8,5): Aspekte einer theologischen Anthropologie*, edited by Michaela Bauks, 114–22. Neukirchen-Vluyn: Neukirchener Theologie, 2008.

Gundry, Robert H. *Soma in Biblical Theology: With Emphasis on Pauline Anthropology*. Grand Rapids, MI: Zondervan, 1988.

Guthrie, George H. "Hebrews." In *Commentary on the New Testament Use of the Old Testament*, edited by G. K. Beale and D. A. Carson, 919–95. Grand Rapids, MI: Baker Academic, 2007.

Halperin, David M. *One Hundred Years of Homosexuality: And Other Essays on Greek Love*. New York: Routledge, 1990.

Hanciles, Jehu. *Beyond Christendom: Globalization, African Migration, and the Transformation of the West*. Maryknoll, NY: Orbis, 2008.

Hartenstein, Friedhelm. "'Und sie erkannten, daß sie nackt waren' (Genesis 3,7). Beobachtungen zur Anthropologie der Paradieserzählung." *Evangelische Theologie* 65 (2005): 277–93.

Hasker, William. *The Emergent Self*. Ithaca, NY: Cornell University Press, 2001.

Haslanger, Sally. "Social Construction: The 'Debunking' Project." In *Socializing Metaphysics: The Nature of Social Reality*, edited by Frederick F. Schmitt, 301–25. Lanham, MD: Rowman and Littlefield, 2003.

Hauerwas, Stanley. *Christian Existence Today: Essays on Church, World, and Living in Between*. Durham, NC: Labyrinth, 1988.

———. *The Peaceable Kingdom: A Primer in Christian Ethics*. Notre Dame: University of Notre Dame Press, 1983.

———. *Truthfulness and Tragedy: Further Investigations in Christian Ethics*. Notre Dame: University of Notre Dame Press, 1989.

Hauerwas, Stanley, and William Willimon. *Resident Aliens: Life in the Christian Colony*. Nashville: Abingdon, 1989.

Herdt, Gilbert H. *Third Sex, Third Gender: Beyond Sexual Dimorphism in Culture and History*. New York: Zone Books, 2003.

Hess, Richard D. *Splitting the Adam: The Usage of Ādām in Genesis I–V*. Leiden: Brill, 1990.

"'Hey Ram' Were Gandhi's Last Words, Says Grandson." *The Times of India*, February 1, 2006. https://timesofindia.indiatimes.com/india/Hey-Ram -were-Gandhis-last-words-says-grandson/articleshow/1395570.cms.

Hill, Daniel. *Affect Regulation Theory: A Clinical Model*. New York: W. W. Norton, 2015.

Hoefer, Herbert E. *Churchless Christianity*. Madras, India: Asian Program for Advancement of Training and Studies India, 1991.

Holstein, James A., and Jaber F. Gubrium. *The Self We Live By: Narrative Identity in a Postmodern World*. Oxford: Oxford University Press, 2014.

Horrell, David G. *Solidarity and Difference: Reading of Paul's Ethics*. 2nd ed. New York: Bloomsbury, 2016.

Hutchens, Joshua Caleb. "Christian Worship in Hebrews 12:28 as Ethical and Exclusive." *Journal of the Evangelical Theological Society* 59, no. 3 (2016): 507–22.

Jacobsen, Knut A. "Three Functions of Hell in the Hindu Traditions." *Numen* 56, no. 2–3 (2009): 385–400.

Janowski, Bernd. "Anerkennung und Gegenseitigkeit: Zum konstellativen Personbegriff des Alten Testaments." In *Der Mensch im alten Israel: Neue Forschungen zur alttestamentlichen Anthropologie*, edited by Bernd Janowski and Kathrin Liess, 181–211. Freiburg: Herder, 2009.

———. *Konfliktgespräche mit Gott: Eine Anthropologie der Psalmen.* 3rd ed. Göttingen: Neukirchener Theologie, 2009.

———. "Konstellative Anthropologie: Zum Begriff der Person im Alten Testament." In *Biblische Anthropologie: Neue Einsichten aus dem Alten Testament*, edited by Christian Frevel, 64–87. Freiburg: Herder, 2010.

———. "Wie Spricht das Alte Testament von 'Personaler Identität'? Ein Antwortversuch." In *Konstruktionen individueller und kollektiver identität (I): Altes Israel/Frühjudentum, Griechische Antike, Neues Testament/ Alte Kirche*, edited by Eberhard Bons and Karin Finsterbusch, 31–61. Göttingen: Vandenhoeck & Ruprecht, 2016.

Jenkins, Richard. *Rethinking Ethnicity: Arguments and Explorations.* London: Sage, 2008.

Johnson, Dru. *Knowledge by Ritual: Biblical Prolegomenon to Sacramental Theology.* Winona Lake, IN: Eisenbrauns, 2016.

Johnson, Luke Timothy. *The Revelatory Body: Theology as Inductive Art.* Grand Rapids, MI: Eerdmans, 2015.

Jones, Barry D. "Book Symposium: Spiritual Formation as If the Church Mattered." *Journal of Spiritual Formation & Soul Care* 1, no. 2 (2008): 232–50.

Jones, Constance A., and James D. Ryan. *Encyclopedia of Hinduism.* Encyclopedia of World Religions. New York: Facts on File, 2007.

Jones, E. Stanley. "Report on the New India." *The Christian Century* 64, no. 18 (1947): 555–56.

Kakar, Sudhir. "Indian-ness: So What Really Makes Indians Indian?" *Little India*, April 2, 2007. https://littleindia.com/indian-ness/.

Kanungo, Pralay. "Hindutva's Fury against Christians in Orissa." *Economics & Political Weekly* 43, no. 37 (September 13, 2008): 16–19.

Käsemann, Ernst K. *Das wandernde Gottesvolk: Eine Untersuchung zum Hebräerbrief.* Göttingen: Vandenhoeck & Ruprecht, 1939.

Katongole, Emmanuel, and Chris Rice. *Reconciling All Things: A Christian Vision for Justice, Peace and Healing.* Downers Grove, IL: InterVarsity Press, 2008.

Keener, Craig S. "Family and Household." In *Dictionary of New Testament Background: A Compendium of Contemporary Biblical Scholarship,* edited by Craig A. Evans and Stanley E. Porter, 353–68. Downers Grove, IL: InterVarsity, 2000.

———. *The Mind of the Spirit: Paul's Approach to Transformed Thinking.* Grand Rapids, MI: Baker Academic, 2016.

Kestly, Theresa A. *The Interpersonal Neurobiology of Play: Brain-Building Interventions for Emotional Well-Being.* New York: W. W. Norton, 2014.

Kinnaman, David, and Gabe Lyons. *UnChristian: What a New Generation Really Thinks about Christianity and Why It Matters.* Grand Rapids, MI: Baker Books, 2007.

Klopfenstein, Martin A. *Scham und Schande nach dem Alten Testament: Eine begriffsgeschichtliche Untersuchung zu den hebräischen Wurzeln bôš, klm und ḥpr.* Zürich: Theologischer Verlag, 1972.

Koester, Craig R. "Hebrews, Rhetoric, and the Future." In *Reading the Epistle to the Hebrews: A Resource for Students,* edited by Eric F. Mason and Kevin B. McCruden, 99–120. Atlanta: Society of Biblical Literature, 2011.

———. *Hebrews: Translation with Introduction and Commentary.* New York: Doubleday, 2001.

Köhler, Ludwig, and Walter Baumgartner. *Hebräisches und Aramäisches Lexikon zum Alten Testament (HALAT).* Edited by Walter Baumgartner, Johann Jakob Stamm, and Benedikt Hartmann. 3rd ed. Vol. 1. Leiden: Brill, 2004.

Lakoff, George, and Mark Johnson. *Philosophy in the Flesh: The Embodied Mind and Its Challenge to Western Thought.* New York: Basic Books, 1999.

Lapsley, Jacqueline E. "Shame and Self-Knowledge: The Positive Role of Shame in Ezekiel's View of the Moral Self." In *The Book of Ezekiel: Theological and Anthropological Perspectives,* edited by Margaret S. Odell and John T. Strong, 143–73. Atlanta: Society of Biblical Literature, 2000.

Lawler, Steph. *Identity: Sociological Perspectives.* Cambridge: Polity, 2014.

Lewis, C. S. *Allegory of Love: In Medieval Tradition.* Oxford: Oxford University Press, 1977.

Lipner, Julius, and George Gispert-Sauch, eds. *The Writings of Brahmabandhab Upadhyay: Including a Resumé of His Life and Thought.* 2 vols. Bangalore, India: United Theological College, 1991.

MacIntyre, Alasdair. *Whose Justice? Which Rationality?* Notre Dame: University of Notre Dame Press, 1989.

Malina, Bruce J. *The New Testament World: Insights from Cultural Anthropology.* Louisville: Westminster John Knox Press, 2001.

Mann, Susan Archer. *Doing Feminist Theory: From Modernity to Postmodernity.* New York: Oxford University Press, 2012.

McAdams, Dan P. *The Person: A New Introduction to Personality Psychology.* Hoboken, NJ: J. Wiley & Sons, 2006.

———. "The Redemptive Self: Narrative Identity in America Today." In *The Self and Memory*, edited by Denise R. Beike, James M. Lampinen, and Douglas A. Behrend, 95–116. New York: Psychology, 2004.

McGill, Jenny. *Religious Identity and Cultural Negotiation: Toward a Theology of Christian Identity in Migration.* Eugene, OR: Pickwick, 2016.

McGrath, Alister E. *Mere Apologetics: How to Help Seekers and Skeptics Find Faith.* Grand Rapids, MI: Baker Books, 2012.

McGuire, Meredith B. "Religion and the Body: Rematerializing the Human Body in the Social Sciences of Religion." *Journal for the Scientific Study of Religion* 29, no. 3 (1990): 283–96.

McVann, Mark. "Family-Centeredness." In *Handbook of Biblical Social Values*, edited by John J. Pilch and Bruce J. Malina, 64–67. Eugene, OR: Cascade, 2016.

Meek, Esther Lightcap. *Loving to Know: Covenant Epistemology.* Eugene, OR: Wipf & Stock, 2011.

Merleau-Ponty, Maurice. *Phenomenology of Perception.* London: Forgotten Books, 2015.

Mikulincer, Mario, and Phillip R. Shaver. *Attachment in Adulthood: Structure, Dynamics, and Change.* 2nd ed. New York: Guilford Press, 2016.

Moltmann, Jürgen. "Theology in the Project of the Modern World." In *A Passion for God's Reign: Theology, Christian Learning and the Christian Self*, edited by Miroslav Volf, 1–22. Grand Rapids, MI: Eerdmans, 1998.

Moreland, J. P., and Scott B. Rae. *Body and Soul: Human Nature and the Crisis in Ethics.* Downers Grove, IL: InterVarsity Press, 2000.

Moya, Paula M. L., and Michael R. Hames-Garcia. *Reclaiming Identity: Realist Theory and the Predicament of Postmodernism.* Berkeley: University of California Press, 2000.

Murphy, Nancey. *Bodies and Souls, or Spirited Bodies?* Cambridge: Cambridge University Press, 2006.

————. "Do Humans Have Souls?: Perspectives from Philosophy, Science, and Religion." *Interpretation* 67, no. 1 (2013): 30–41. https://doi.org /10.1177/0020964312463192.

Musekura, Célestin. *An Assessment of Contemporary Models of Forgiveness.* New York: Peter Lang, 2010.

Nel, Philip J. "בוש." In *The New International Dictionary of Old Testament Theology and Exegesis*, edited by Willem A. Vangemeren, 612–18. Grand Rapids, MI: Zondervan, 1997.

Öhler, Markus. "Identität—Eine Problemanzeige." In *Religionsgemeinschaft und Identität: Prozesse jüdischer und christlicher Identitätsbildung im Rahmen der Antike*, edited by Markus Öhler, 9–15. Neukirchen-Vluyn: Neukirchener Theologie, 2013.

Owens, Timothy J. "Self and Identity." In *Handbook of Social Psychology*, edited by John D. DeLamater, 205–32. New York: Kluwer Academic/ Plenum, 2003.

Owens, Timothy J., and Sarah Samblanet. "Self and Self-Concept." In *Handbook of Social Psychology*, edited by John D. DeLamater and Amanda Ward, 225–49. New York: Springer, 2013.

Pak, Jenny Hyun Chung. *Korean American Women: Stories of Acculturation and Changing Selves.* New York: Routledge, 2006.

Park, Jerry Z. "The Ethnic and Religious Identities of Young Asian Americans." PhD diss., University of Notre Dame, 2004.

Peterson, Eugene. "Spirituality for All the Wrong Reasons." *Christianity Today* 49, no. 3 (2005): 42–48.

Pinkney, Andrea Marion. "Prasāda, the Gracious Gift, in Contemporary and Classical South Asia." *Journal of the American Academy of Religion* 81, no. 3 (2013): 734–56.

Pittman, Joe F., Margaret K. Keiley, Jennifer L. Kerpelman, and Brian E. Vaughn. "Attachment, Identity, and Intimacy: Parallels between Bowlby's and Erikson's Paradigms." *Journal of Family Theory and Review* 3, no. 1 (2011): 32–46. https://doi.org/10.1111/j.1756-2589.2010.00079.x.

Polanyi, Michael. *Personal Knowledge: Towards a Post-Critical Philosophy.* Chicago: University of Chicago Press, 1974.

Polanyi, Michael, and Amartya Sen. *The Tacit Dimension.* Chicago: University of Chicago Press, 2009.

Prokes, Mary Timothy. *Toward a Theology of the Body.* Grand Rapids, MI: Eerdmans, 1996.

Pyne, Robert A. "Created in the Image of God." In *Understanding Christian Theology*, edited by Charles R. Swindoll and Roy B. Zuck, 673–84. Nashville: Thomas Nelson, 2003.

———. *Humanity and Sin: The Creation, Fall, and Redemption of Humanity*. Nashville: Thomas Nelson, 1999.

Rambachan, Anantanand. "Seeing the Divine in All Forms: The Culmination of Hindu Worship." *Dialogue and Alliance* 4, no. 1 (Spring 1990): 5–12.

Rapske, Brian M. "Citizenship, Roman." In *Dictionary of New Testament Background: A Compendium of Contemporary Biblical Scholarship*, edited by Craig A. Evans and Stanley E. Porter, 215–18. Downers Grove, IL: InterVarsity, 2000.

Ratner, Kaylin. "The Role of Parenting and Attachment in Identity Style Development." *The University of Central Florida Undergraduate Research Journal* 7, no. 1 (2017): 15–26. https://www.urj.ucf.edu/docs/ratner.pdf.

Robinson, John A. T. *The Body*. London: Hymns Ancient & Modern, 2012.

Rogerson, John W. "The Hebrew Conception of Corporate Personality: A Re-Examination." In *Anthropological Approaches to the Old Testament*, edited by Bernhard Lang, 43–59. Philadelphia: Fortress Press, 1985.

"Roop Committed Sati of Her Own Free Will." *The Indian Post*, December 15, 1988.

Runge, Steven E. *Discourse Grammar of the Greek New Testament: A Practical Introduction for Teaching and Exegesis*. Peabody, MA: Hendrickson, 2011.

Samuel, Dibin. "Wiliam Carey Played Significant Role in Abolishing Sati System." *Christian Today*, December 4, 2009. http://www.christiantoday .co.in/article/wiliam.carey.played.significant.role.in.abolishing.sati.system /4906.htm.

Santrock, John W. *Lifespan Development*. 15th ed. New York: McGraw Hill Education, 2015.

Schore, Allan, and Judith Schore. *The Science of the Art of Psychotherapy*. New York: W. W. Norton, 2012.

Schroer, Silvia, and Thomas Staubli. *Body Symbolism in the Bible*. Collegeville, MN: Liturgical Press, 2001.

Sedmak, Clemens. *The Capacity to Be Displaced: Resilience, Mission, and Inner Strength*. Boston: Brill, 2017.

Seebaß, Horst. *Genesis I: Urgeschichte (1,1–11,26)*. Neukirchen-Vluyn: Neukirchener Theologie, 1996.

————. "Israels Identität als Volk des Einen Gottes." In *Religion und Identität: Im Horizont des Pluralismus*, edited by Werner Gephardt and Hans Waldenfels, 87–104. Frankfurt: Suhrkamp, 1999.

————. "בושׁ." In *Theologisches Wörterbuch zum Alten Testament* (*THWAT*), edited by G. Johannes Botterweck, Helmer Ringgren, and Heinz-Josef Fabry, 568–80. Stuttgart: Kohlhammer, 1973.

Shukla, Vandana. "Hindu Women and Property: Myth versus Reality." *The Tribune*, September 12, 2015. http://www.tribuneindia.com/news/comment /hindu-women-property-myth-vs-reality/131896.html.

Siegel, Daniel J. *Brainstorm: The Power and Purpose of the Teenage Brain*. New York: Bantam Books, 2013.

————. *The Developing Mind: How Relationships and the Brain Interact to Shape Who We Are*. 2nd ed. New York: Guilford Press, 2015.

————. *The Mindful Brain Reflection and Attunement in the Cultivation of Well-Being*. New York: W. W. Norton, 2007.

————. *Mindsight: The New Science of Personal Transformation*. New York: Bantam Books, 2011.

Siegel, Daniel J., and Mary Hartzell. *Parenting from the Inside Out: How a Deeper Self Understanding Can Help You Raise Children Who Thrive*. New York: Penguin Group, 2003.

Smith, Christian. *What Is a Person?: Rethinking Humanity, Social Life, and the Moral Good from the Person Up*. Chicago: University of Chicago Press, 2011.

Smith, James K. A. *How (Not) to Be Secular: Reading Charles Taylor*. Grand Rapids, MI: Eerdmans, 2014.

————. *You Are What You Love: The Spiritual Power of Habit*. Grand Rapids, MI: Brazos Press, 2016.

Snodgrass, Klyne. "Introduction to a Hermeneutics of Identity." *Bibliotheca Sacra* 168, no. 669 (January–March 2011): 3–19.

————. "Paul's Focus on Identity." *Bibliotheca Sacra* 168, no. 671 (July–September 2011): 259–73.

Spurgeon, Andrew B. *Twin Cultures Separated by Centuries: An Indian Reading of 1 Corinthians*. Carlisle, UK: Langham Global Library, 2016.

Srivastava, Piyush. "'We Will Free India of Muslims and Christians by 2021': DJS Leader Vows to Continue 'Ghar Wapsi' Plans and Restore 'Hindu Glory.'" *Daily Mail*, December 18, 2014. http://www.dailymail.co.uk /indiahome/indianews/article-2879597/We-free-India-Muslims-Christians -2021-DJS-leader-vows-continue-ghar-wapsi-plans-restore-Hindu-glory .html.

Stansell, Gary. "Honor and Shame in the David Narratives." *Semeia* 68 (1996): 55–79.

Stolz, F. "בוש." In *Theological Lexicon of the Old Testament*, edited by Ernst Jenni and Claus Westermann, 204–7. Peabody, MA: Hendrickson Publishers, 1997.

Streeter, Burnett Hillman, and Aiyadurai Jesudasen Appasamy. *The Sadhu: A Study in Mysticism and Practical Religion.* London: Macmillan, 1921.

Strong, James. *New Strong's Exhaustive Concordance.* Nashville: Thomas Nelson, 2003.

Susin, Luiz Carlos. "A Critique of the Identity Paradigm." In *Creating Identity*, edited by Hermann Häring, Maureen Mieth, and Dietmar Junker-Kenny, 78–90. London: SCM, 2000.

Taylor, Charles. "The Politics of Recognition." In *Multiculturalism: Examining the Politics of Recognition*, edited by Charles Taylor and Amy Gutmann, 25–74. Princeton: Princeton University Press, 1994.

———. *Sources of the Self: The Making of the Modern Identity.* Cambridge, MA: Harvard University Press, 1989.

Thompson, Curt. *Anatomy of the Soul: Surprising Connections between Neuroscience and Spiritual Practices That Can Transform Your Life and Relationships.* Carol Stream, IL: Tyndale House Publishers, 2010.

———. *Soul of Shame: Retelling the Stories We Believe about Ourselves.* Downers Grove, IL: InterVarsity Press, 2015.

Thompson, James W. "Insider Ethics for Outsiders: Ethics for Aliens in Hebrews." *Restoration Quarterly* 53, no. 4 (2011): 207–19.

Ticciati, Susannah. *Job and the Disruption of Identity: Reading beyond Barth.* London: T&T Clark, 2005.

Tozer, A. W. *Knowledge of the Holy: The Attributes of God.* San Francisco: HarperOne, 2009.

Trebilco, Paul. *Self-Designations and Group Identity in the New Testament.* New York: Cambridge University Press, 2012.

Turner, Jonathan H. *Contemporary Sociological Theory.* Los Angeles: Sage, 2013.

Vanhoozer, Kevin J. *The Drama of Doctrine: A Canonical Linguistic Approach to Christian Doctrine.* Louisville: Westminster John Knox, 2005.

Vanhoye, Père Albert. "La Question Littéraire De Hébreux xiii. 1–6." *New Testament Studies* 23, no. 2 (1977): 121–39.

Varma, Pavan K. *Being Indian: Inside the Real India.* London: Arrow Books, 2006.

Volf, Miroslav. *After Our Likeness: The Church as the Image of the Trinity*. Grand Rapids, MI: Eerdmans, 1998.

———. "Being as God Is." In *God's Life in Trinity*, edited by Miroslav Volf and Michael Welker, 3–12. Minneapolis: Fortress Press, 2006.

———. *The End of Memory: Remembering Rightly in a Violent World*. Grand Rapids, MI: Eerdmans, 2006.

———. *Exclusion and Embrace: A Theological Exploration of Identity, Otherness, and Reconciliation*. Nashville: Abingdon, 1996.

von Rad, Gerhard. *Das erste Buch Mose: Genesis*. Vol. 9. Göttingen: Vandenhoeck & Ruprecht, 1972.

Wells, Samuel. *Improvisation: The Drama of Christian Ethics*. Grand Rapids, MI: Brazos Press, 2004.

Westermann, Claus. *Genesis*. Neukirchen-Vluyn: Neukirchener Verlag, 1974.

Willard, Dallas. *Renovation of the Heart: Putting on the Character of Christ*. Colorado Springs: NavPress, 2002.

Williams, A. N. "Assimilation and Otherness: The Theological Significance of Négritude." *International Journal of Systematic Theology* 11, no. 3 (2009): 248–70.

Wilson, Margaret. "Six Views of Embodied Cognition." *Psychonomic Bulletin and Review* 9, no. 4 (2002): 625–36. https://doi.org/10.3758/bf03196322.

Wittig, Monique. *The Straight Mind and Other Essays*. Boston: Beacon, 1992.

Wolff, Hans Walter. *Anthropology of the Old Testament*. 2nd ed. London: SCM Press, 2012.

Wright, N. T. *Surprised by Hope: Rethinking Heaven, the Resurrection, and the Mission of the Church*. New York: HarperOne, 2008.

Yocum, Glenn E. "Burning 'Widows,' Sacred 'Prostitutes,' and 'Perfect Wives': Recent Studies of Hindu Women." *Religious Studies Review* 20, no. 4 (1994): 277–85.

About the Contributors

Marc-André Caron, having grown up in Québec, where evangelical Christianity represents less than 0.5 percent of the population, has a passion to communicate the message of the Old and New Testaments with accuracy and precision to shape worldviews. He serves as an associate pastor in Église Évangélique de Chicoutimi and is a PhD student in New Testament at Université Laval in Québec.

Nate Collins (PhD, Southern Baptist Theological Seminary) is the Founder and President of Revoice, an organization that supports, encourages, and empowers Christian gender and sexual minorities so they can flourish while adhering to the historic, Christian doctrine of marriage and sexuality. Nate specializes in theological and intercultural dialogue on the subject of gender and sexuality and is the author of *All But Invisible: Exploring Identity Questions at the Intersection of Faith, Gender, and Sexuality.*

Lisa Igram is the Associate Dean of Spiritual Development at Biola University, where she enjoys teaching and training undergraduates in the areas of discipleship, spiritual formation, and leadership. Her career in higher education has led her from teaching in China to developing and managing programming for international students in the United States and to her current role of aiding in the oversight of campus ministry programming at Biola University. A trained Spiritual Director and member of the Evangelical Spiritual Director's Association (ESDA), Lisa is currently pursuing a PhD in Divinity and Religious Studies at the University of Aberdeen.

Jenny McGill (PhD, King's College London) currently serves as Regional Dean at Indiana Wesleyan University and as an adjunct faculty member of Dallas Theological Seminary. A Fulbright award recipient, she has worked in international education and intercultural training with clients and students from more than sixty nations. She is the author of *Religious Identity and Cultural Negotiation* and *Walk with Me*, among other published works. Travel for community service, teaching, and research has taken her to thirty countries on six continents.

Célestin Musekura (PhD, Theological Studies, Dallas Theological Seminary) is an international speaker and the president and founder of African Leadership and Reconciliation Ministries (ALARM Inc.). An ordained Baptist minister who was born and raised in Rwanda, he specializes in communal forgiveness, servant leadership, and justice administration. He travels consistently to East and Central Africa, training leaders in peace-building, biblical forgiveness, and tribal reconciliation. He has written *Forgiving as We've Been Forgiven* (with Gregory Jones) and *Assessment of Contemporary Models of Forgiveness* and coedited *Restoring the Beauty and Blessing of Ethnic Diversity* (with Andy Alo), among other works.

Rod Reed (PhD in Theology, University of Bristol) has, over the past twenty years, served two universities as chaplain, administrator, and professor of theology. He is currently serving as Dean of Christian Formation and Associate Professor of Theology at John Brown University. He has also served as a research consultant to nearly thirty Christian universities across the globe to assess their processes of spiritual formation. He is the coeditor of *Building a Culture of Faith: University-Wide Partnerships for Spiritual Formation* and speaks regularly at conferences and universities.

Jürgen Schulz is a German pastor, lecturer, and PhD candidate at the Evangelische Theologische Faculteit in Leuven, Belgium. He obtained his theological education in Germany and the United States. He currently serves as the pastor of a church that he planted in downtown Paderborn, Germany. Besides pastoral ministry, he immerses himself in academic work. He teaches as a guest lecturer at various institutions and is currently completing his dissertation on the concept of shame in the ancient Near Eastern context and the Hebrew Testament.

Andrew B. Spurgeon (PhD, New Testament Studies, Dallas Theological Seminary), a native of India, serves as Professor at Singapore Bible College. Andrew has also taught at universities, seminaries, and churches in India, Nepal, Sri Lanka, the Philippines, and the United States. He is the publications chairperson for the Asia Theological Association and one of the New Testament editors for the *Asia Bible Commentary Series*. His latest book is *Twin Cultures Separated by Centuries: An Indian Reading of 1 Corinthians*.

Andi Thacker is Assistant Professor of Biblical Counseling at Dallas Theological Seminary. In addition to her teaching responsibilities, Andi maintains a small private practice in which she specializes with children and adolescents and supervises licensed professional counselor interns. Dr. Thacker obtained a PhD in counselor education and supervision from the University of North Texas. She is a licensed professional and nationally certified counselor, a board-approved supervisor, and a registered play therapist supervisor.